DIANE LINDSEY REEVES
WITH
NANCY HEUBECK

Illustrations by
NANCY BOND

Facts On File, Inc.

CAREER IDEAS FOR KIDS WHO LIKE ADVENTURE

Checkmark Books
An imprint of Facts On File, Inc.
11 Penn Plaza
New York NY 10001

Library of Congress Cataloging-in-Publication Data

Reeves, Diane Lindsey, 1959–
    Career ideas for kids who like adventure / Diane Lindsey Reeves with
Nancy Heubeck; illustrations by Nancy Bond.
        p.   cm. — (Career ideas for kids who like)
    Includes bibliographical references and index.
    ISBN 0-8160-4321-3 (hardcover) — ISBN 0-8160-4322-1 (pbk.)
        1. Vocational guidance—Juvenile literature. 2. Adventure and
adventurers—Vocational guidance—Juvenile literature. [1. Adventure
and adventurers—Vocational guidance. 2. Vocational guidance.]
Heubeck, Nancy. II. Bond, Nancy, ill. III. Title.

HF5381.2.R428 2001
331.7'02—dc21
                                                                00-055108

Checkmark Books are available at special discounts when purchased in bulk
quantities for businesses, associations, institutions, or sales promotions.
Please call our Special Sales Department in New York at 212/967-8800 or
800/322-8755.

You can find Facts On File on the World Wide Web at http://www.factsonfile.com

Text and cover design by Smart Graphics
Illustrations by Nancy Bond

This book is printed on acid-free paper.

Printed in the United States of America

MP FOF 10 9 8 7 6 5 4 3 2 1

(pbk)   10 9 8 7 6 5 4 3 2 1

CONTENTS

A million thanks to those who took the time to invest in young lives by sharing their stories about work and providing photos for this book:

Roy Clark
Cary R. Cooley
Coby Croft
Martha Culp
Kadri Dagdelen
Sarah Gordon
Joan E. Higginbotham
Tracee Kelly
Kandy Knott
David W. Lawrence
Aaron Marcus
Alan W. Neil
Dan Petit
Earl M. Walker, Jr.
Paula Washow

Special thanks to the publishing team at Facts On File for their incredible work on behalf of this series: Laurie Likoff, Kate Moore, Lisa Milberg, Linda Leonard, Paul Conklin, Beth Shindler, Terence Maikels, and especially my editor, Nicole Bowen. It's been great fun working with all of you!

MAKE A CHOICE!

You're young. Most of your life is still ahead of you. How are you supposed to know what you want to be when you grow up?

You're right: 10, 11, 12, 13 is a bit young to know exactly what and where and how you're going to do whatever it is you're going to do as an adult. But, it's the perfect time to start making some important discoveries about who you are, what you like to do, and what you do best. It's the ideal time to start thinking about what you *want* to do.

Make a choice! If you get a head start now, you may avoid setbacks and mistakes later on.

When it comes to picking a career, you've basically got two choices.

CHOICE A

Wait until you're in college to start figuring out what you want to do. Even then you still may not decide what's up your alley, so you graduate and jump from job to job still searching for something you really like.

Hey, it could work. It might be fun. Lots of (probably most) people do it this way.

The problem is that if you pick Choice A, you may end up settling for second best. You may miss out on a meaningful education, satisfying work, and the rewards of a focused and well-planned career.

You have another choice to consider.

CHOICE B

Start now figuring out your options and thinking about the things that are most important in your life's work: Serving others? Staying true to your values? Making lots of money? Enjoying your work? Your young years are the perfect time to mess around with different career ideas without messing up your life.

Reading this book is a great idea for kids who choose B. It's a first step toward choosing a career that matches your skills, interests, and lifetime goals. It will help you make a plan for tailoring your junior and high school years to fit your career dreams. To borrow a jingle from the U.S. Army—using this book is a way to discover how to "be all that you can be."

Ready for the challenge of Choice B? If so, read the next section to find out how this book can help start you on your way.

HOW TO USE THIS BOOK

This isn't a book about interesting careers that other people have. It's a book about interesting careers that you can have.

Of course, it won't do you a bit of good to just read this book. To get the whole shebang, you're going to have to jump in with both feet, roll up your sleeves, put on your thinking cap—whatever it takes—to help you do these three things:

- ☀ **Discover** what you do best and enjoy the most. (This is the secret ingredient for finding work that's perfect for you.)

- ☼ **Explore** ways to match your interests and abilities with career ideas.
- ☼ **Experiment** with lots of different ideas until you find the ideal career. (It's like trying on all kinds of hats to see which ones fit!)

Use this book as a road map to some exciting career destinations. Here's what to expect in the chapters that follow.

GET IN GEAR!

First stop: self-discovery. These activities will help you uncover important clues about the special traits and abilities that make you *you*. When you are finished you will have developed a personal Skill Set that will help guide you to career ideas in the next chapter.

TAKE A TRIP!

Next stop: exploration. Cruise down the career idea highway and find out about a variety of career ideas that are especially appropriate for people who like adventure. Use the Skill Set chart at the beginning of each entry to match your own interests with those required for success on the job.

MAKE AN ADVENTURE-FILLED DETOUR!

Here's your chance to explore all kinds of exciting careers that are jam-packed with adventure.

Just when you thought you'd have to sit at a desk for the rest of your life, here come dozens of new ideas to get you out exploring the world and making a difference. Charge up your career search by learning all you can about some of these opportunities.

DON'T STOP NOW!

Third stop: experimentation. The library, the telephone, a computer, and a mentor—four keys to a successful career planning adventure. Use them well, and before long you'll be on the trail of some hot career ideas.

WHAT'S NEXT?

Make a plan! Chart your course (or at least the next stop) with these career planning road maps. Whether you're moving full steam ahead with a great idea or get slowed down at a yellow light of indecision, these road maps will keep you moving forward toward a great future.

Use a pencil—you're bound to make a detour or two along the way. But, hey, you've got to start somewhere.

HOORAY! YOU DID IT!

Some final rules of the road before sending you off to new adventures.

SOME FUTURE DESTINATIONS

This section lists a few career planning tools you'll want to know about.

You've got a lot of ground to cover in this phase of your career planning journey. Start your engines and get ready for an exciting adventure!

Career planning is a lifelong journey. There's usually more than one way to get where you're going, and there are often some interesting detours along the way. But, you have to start somewhere. So, rev up and find out all you can about you—one-of-a-kind, specially designed you. That's the first stop on what can be the most exciting trip of your life!

To get started, complete the two exercises described below.

WATCH FOR SIGNS ALONG THE WAY

Road signs help drivers figure out how to get where they want to go. They provide clues about direction, road conditions, and safety. Your career road signs will provide clues about who you are, what you like, and what you do best. These clues can help you decide where to look for the career ideas that are best for you.

Complete the following statements to make them true for you. There are no right or wrong answers. Jot down the response that describes you best. Your answers will provide important clues about career paths you should explore.

Please Note: If this book does not belong to you, write your responses on a separate sheet of paper.

On my last report card, I got the best grade in _____ .

On my last report card, I got the worst grade in _____ .

I am happiest when _____ .

Something I can do for hours without getting bored is _____ .

Something that bores me out of my mind is _____ .

My favorite class is _____ .

My least favorite class is _____ .

The one thing I'd like to accomplish with my life is _____ .

My favorite thing to do after school is _ .

My least favorite thing to do after school is _____ .

Something I'm really good at is _____ .

Something that is really tough for me to do is _____ .

My favorite adult person is _____ because _____ .

When I grow up _____ .

The kinds of books I like to read are about _____ .

The kinds of videos I like to watch are about _____ .

GET SOME DIRECTION

It's easy to get lost when you don't have a good idea of where you want to go. This is especially true when you start thinking about what to do with the rest of your life. Unless you focus on where you want to go, you might get lost or even miss the exit. This second exercise will help you connect your own interests and abilities with a whole world of career opportunities.

Mark the activities that you enjoy doing or would enjoy doing if you had the chance. Be picky. Don't mark ideas that you wish you would do, mark only those that you would really do. For instance, if the idea of skydiving sounds appealing, but you'd never do it because you are terrified of heights, don't mark it.

Please Note: If this book does not belong to you, write your responses on a separate sheet of paper.

❏ 1. Rescue a cat stuck in a tree
❏ 2. Visit the pet store every time you go to the mall
❏ 3. Paint a mural on the cafeteria wall
❏ 4. Send e-mail to a "pen pal" in another state
❏ 5. Survey your classmates to find out what they do after school
❏ 6. Run for student council
❏ 7. Try out for the school play
❏ 8. Dissect a frog and identify the different organs
❏ 9. Play baseball, soccer, football, or _____ (fill in your favorite sport)

❏ 10. Talk on the phone to just about anyone who will talk back

❏ 11. Try foods from all over the world—Thailand, Poland, Japan, etc.

❏ 12. Write poems about things that are happening in your life

❏ 13. Create a really scary haunted house to take your friends through on Halloween

❏ 14. Recycle all your family's trash

❏ 15. Bake a cake and decorate it for your best friend's birthday

❏ 16. Simulate an imaginary flight through space on your computer screen

❏ 17. Build model airplanes, boats, doll houses, or anything from kits

❏ 18. Sell enough advertisements for the school yearbook to win a trip to Walt Disney World

❏ 19. Teach your friends a new dance routine

❏ 20. Watch the stars come out at night and see how many constellations you can find

❏ 21. Watch baseball, soccer, football, or _____ (fill in your favorite sport) on TV

❏ 22. Give a speech in front of the entire school

❏ 23. Plan the class field trip to Washington, D.C.

❏ 24. Read everything in sight, including the back of the cereal box

❏ 25. Figure out "who dunnit" in a mystery story

❏ 26. Take in stray or hurt animals

❏ 27. Make a poster announcing the school football game

❏ 28. Put together a multimedia show for a school assembly using music and lots of pictures and graphics

❏ 29. Think up a new way to make the lunch line move faster and explain it to the cafeteria staff

❏ 30. Invest your allowance in the stock market and keep track of how it does

❏ 31. Go to the ballet or opera every time you get the chance

❏ 32. Do experiments with a chemistry set

❏ 33. Keep score at your sister's Little League game

❏ 34. Use lots of funny voices when reading stories to children

❏ 35. Ride on airplanes, trains, boats—anything that moves

❏ 36. Interview the new exchange student for an article in the school newspaper

❏ 37. Build your own treehouse

❏ 38. Help clean up a waste site in your neighborhood

❏ 39. Visit an art museum and pick out your favorite painting

❏ 40. Make a chart on the computer to show how much soda students buy from the school vending machines each week

❏ 41. Keep track of how much your team earns to buy new uniforms

❏ 42. Play Monopoly® in an all-night championship challenge

❏ 43. Play an instrument in the school band or orchestra

❏ 44. Put together a 1,000-piece puzzle

❏ 45. Write stories about sports for the school newspaper

❏ 46. Listen to other people talk about their problems

❏ 47. Imagine yourself in exotic places

❏ 48. Hang around bookstores and libraries

❏ 49. Play harmless practical jokes on April Fools' Day

❑ 50. Join the 4-H club at your school
❑ 51. Take photographs at the school talent show
❑ 52. Create an imaginary city using a computer
❑ 53. Do 3-D puzzles
❑ 54. Make money by setting up your own business—paper route, lemonade stand, etc.
❑ 55. Keep track of the top 10 songs of the week
❑ 56. Train your dog to do tricks
❑ 57. Make play-by-play announcements at the school football game
❑ 58. Answer the phones during a telethon to raise money for orphans
❑ 59. Be an exchange student in another country
❑ 60. Write down all your secret thoughts and favorite sayings in a journal
❑ 61. Jump out of an airplane (with a parachute, of course)
❑ 62. Plant and grow a garden in your backyard (or windowsill)
❑ 63. Use a video camera to make your own movies
❑ 64. Spend your summer at a computer camp learning lots of new computer programs
❑ 65. Build bridges, skyscrapers, and other structures out of LEGO®s

❑ 66. Get your friends together to help clean up your town after a hurricane

❑ 67. Plan a concert in the park for little kids

❑ 68. Collect different kinds of rocks

❑ 69. Help plan a sports tournament

❑ 70. Be DJ for the school dance

❑ 71. Learn how to fly a plane or sail a boat

❑ 72. Write funny captions for pictures in the school yearbook

❑ 73. Scuba dive to search for buried treasure

❑ 74. Recognize and name several different breeds of cats, dogs, and other animals

❑ 75. Sketch pictures of your friends

❑ 76. Answer your classmates' questions about how to use the computer

❑ 77. Draw a map showing how to get to your house from school

❑ 78. Pick out neat stuff to sell at the school store

❑ 79. Make up new words to your favorite songs

❑ 80. Take a hike and name the different kinds of trees, birds, or flowers

❑ 81. Referee intramural basketball games

❑ 82. Join the school debate team

❑ 83. Make a poster with postcards from all the places you went on your summer vacation

❑ 84. Write down stories that your grandparents tell you about when they were young

CALCULATE THE CLUES

Now is your chance to add it all up. Each of the 12 boxes on these pages contains an interest area that is common to both your world and the world of work. Follow these directions to discover your personal Skill Set:

1. Find all of the numbers that you checked on pages 9–13 in the boxes below and X them. Work your way all the way through number 84.
2. Go back and count the Xs marked for each interest area. Write that number in the space that says "total."
3. Find the interest area with the highest total and put a number one in the "Rank" blank of that box. Repeat this process for the next two highest scoring areas. Rank the second highest as number two and the third highest as number three.
4. If you have more than three strong areas, choose the three that are most important and interesting to you.

Remember: If this book does not belong to you, write your responses on a separate sheet of paper.

ADVENTURE
- ❏ 1
- ❏ 13
- ❏ 25
- ❏ 37
- ❏ 49
- ❏ 61
- ❏ 73
- Total: _____
- Rank: _____

ANIMALS & NATURE
- ❏ 2
- ❏ 14
- ❏ 26
- ❏ 38
- ❏ 50
- ❏ 62
- ❏ 74
- Total: _____
- Rank: _____

ART
- ❏ 3
- ❏ 15
- ❏ 27
- ❏ 39
- ❏ 51
- ❏ 63
- ❏ 75
- Total: _____
- Rank: _____

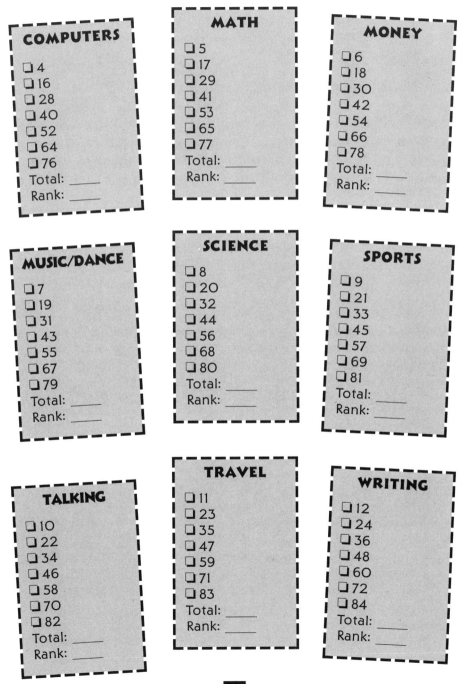

COMPUTERS

☐ 4
☐ 16
☐ 28
☐ 40
☐ 52
☐ 64
☐ 76
Total: _____
Rank: _____

MATH

☐ 5
☐ 17
☐ 29
☐ 41
☐ 53
☐ 65
☐ 77
Total: _____
Rank: _____

MONEY

☐ 6
☐ 18
☐ 30
☐ 42
☐ 54
☐ 66
☐ 78
Total: _____
Rank: _____

MUSIC/DANCE

☐ 7
☐ 19
☐ 31
☐ 43
☐ 55
☐ 67
☐ 79
Total: _____
Rank: _____

SCIENCE

☐ 8
☐ 20
☐ 32
☐ 44
☐ 56
☐ 68
☐ 80
Total: _____
Rank: _____

SPORTS

☐ 9
☐ 21
☐ 33
☐ 45
☐ 57
☐ 69
☐ 81
Total: _____
Rank: _____

TALKING

☐ 10
☐ 22
☐ 34
☐ 46
☐ 58
☐ 70
☐ 82
Total: _____
Rank: _____

TRAVEL

☐ 11
☐ 23
☐ 35
☐ 47
☐ 59
☐ 71
☐ 83
Total: _____
Rank: _____

WRITING

☐ 12
☐ 24
☐ 36
☐ 48
☐ 60
☐ 72
☐ 84
Total: _____
Rank: _____

What are your top three interest areas? List them here (or on a separate piece of paper).

1. _____
2. _____
3. _____

This is your personal Skill Set and provides important clues about the kinds of work you're most likely to enjoy. Remember it and look for career ideas with a skill set that matches yours most closely.

TAKE A TRIP!

Cruise down the
career idea highway and
enjoy in-depth profiles of some of the interesting options in
this field. Keep in mind all that you've discovered about
yourself so far. Find the careers that match your own Skill
Set first. After that, keep on trucking through the other
ideas—exploration is the name of this game.

Challenge, daring, and going far beyond the call of duty
are common ingredients in adventurous careers. They're
not for everyone. But true adventure lovers wouldn't have
it any other way.

Many of these careers require much more physical sta-
mina than a "regular" job. Others require testing boundaries

and reaching new heights. Quite often the warmth and security of an office is replaced by work in the great outdoors.

Adventure-packed careers can be good choices for people who shudder at the thought of a nine-to-five job. They can also provide meaningful ways to make a difference and help others. Most are high on challenge and low on boredom.

Do you want a career with on-the-job training? Want to see the world while you work? Take a look at some of the careers that follow and get ready for the adventure of your life!

Also, as you read about the following careers, imagine yourself doing each job and ask yourself the following questions:

- ☼ Would I like it?
- ☼ Would I be good at it?
- ☼ Is it the stuff my career dreams are made of?

If so, make a quick exit to explore what it involves, try it out, check it out, and get acquainted!

Buckle up and enjoy the trip!

A NOTE ON WEBSITES

Internet sites tend to move around the Web a bit. If you have trouble finding a particular site, use an Internet browser to find a specific website or type of information.

TAKE A TRIP!

Airplane Pilot

SHORTCUTS

GO fly a kite.

READ Charles Lindbergh's account of the first nonstop transatlantic flight from New York to Paris in *The Spirit of St. Louis* (Minneapolis: Minnesota Historical Society, 1954).

TRY building a model airplane.

SKILL SET

✔ ADVENTURE

✔ TRAVEL

✔ MATH

WHAT IS AN AIRPLANE PILOT?

Next time you see a plane flying overhead, consider where it is going. It's flying high and fast, full of people or mail or cargo. How in the world does an airplane stay up there? When there are no road signs and no traffic lights, just the big, open sky, how does a pilot ever find his or her way from one place to another—across cities and towns, rivers and oceans, mountains and skyscrapers?

All that is just part of the thrill of being a pilot. Whether it's an airline pilot flying a planeload of travelers across the country, a military pilot flying a jet into enemy territory, or a charter pilot just doing his or her own thing, they each need skill and daring to get where they want to go.

Small planes usually require just one pilot, but most of the larger ones require two pilots to fly them: the captain, who's in charge of the flight, and a copilot, who helps keep everything on track. Some planes also carry a third pilot called a flight engineer who does most of the navigation tasks and monitors mechanical systems in the aircraft.

Before getting airborne, pilots have to learn how to fly the specific type of plane that they want to fly. While the basic principles of flying may remain consistent from plane to plane, there are so many variations found in different kinds of airplanes that pilots are required to undergo special training

for every type of plane they fly. Depending upon the size and complexity of the airplane, that training could involve a couple of hours or several weeks or months to master each control system. Although computers on modern jets handle many of the technical aspects of flying, the pilot still has to tell the computers what to do and where to go.

Once a plane is in the air, it's a long way down to the ground. That makes safety a pilot's number-one concern. That means that knowing how to fly an airplane is not enough. Pilots need to know their aircraft—inside and out. One of the first things a pilot learns is how a plane flies—what gets it going and keeps it up in the air. They also learn about how such things as weather atmosphere, altitude, and the mechanical workings of a plane can affect a plane in the air. Map reading and navigational skills are essential, so math skills come in handy.

Think it's annoying that you have to tell your parents where you're going when you leave the house? Imagine what it's like to be a pilot. Every time a pilot takes off, he or she has to file a written report with the Federal Aviation Administration (FAA). The FAA has to know where the plane is going, what direction it will take, how long it will fly in that direction, when the pilot will check in along the way, and where—as well as what time—the pilot plans to get there. Talk about the third degree! And that's not all. Once in the air, pilots have to touch base with air traffic controllers every few minutes to tell them where the plane is. And you thought you had it rough!

In the United States, pilots must have a license to fly any type of airplane. It's a lot like a driver's license for a car, but it requires quite a bit more education and practical experience. The test to get the license is a lot harder, too. The basic license—a private pilot's license—is the first step. It allows pilots to fly small planes, but only if they can see clearly for a certain distance. Flying at night or in poor weather conditions requires an instrument license. Airline pilots, or pilots that fly for hire, must have a commercial license, which requires a lot more time in training.

The type of plane a pilot flies often determines what kind of pilot he or she is. A private pilot is someone who has that first, basic license and usually flies a smaller airplane. An airline pilot flies for the commercial airlines, transporting packages, mail, and people. But there are many other kinds of pilots: bush pilots who fly into remote areas where there aren't any airports and land on lakes, rivers, pastures, and just about anywhere to deliver supplies and transport passengers; helicopter pilots who fly helicopters such as the ones that pick up accident victims and fly them to hospitals; crop duster pilots who apply chemicals to farm land to kill insects, fertilize crops, or sow seed; and test pilots who fly new types of airplanes. Military pilots may fly sleek, ultrafast fighter jets, or big, cumbersome cargo planes, or even helicopters as they carry out the missions of the armed forces. A glider pilot flies a plane without an engine and instead uses changes in airflow to move forward, up, or down.

You can earn a private pilot's license by taking a few lessons and getting the required experience at your local airport. To do so, you must meet minimum age and physical requirements to be able to fly alone. You must also pass a written test on basic airplane knowledge, weather patterns, math, government flight regulations, and mechanics. To become an airline pilot, you don't have to have a college education, but it can give you an edge over the competition. You will, however, need to be selected for special training by an airline, which means you have to know what you are doing.

The sky is the limit for adventurous types who want to see the world and love the thrill of taking off into the wide, blue yonder.

TRY IT OUT

BUILD YOUR OWN

Try building your own model airplane. Options range from simple balsa wood planes to sophisticated, radio-controlled jets. Do a search for airplanes at http://www.etoys.com to find just what you are looking for.

And don't overlook that all-time favorite, the paper airplane. For tips on how to make one that will really whiz, try some of the ideas found in books like:

The Best Paper Airplanes You'll Ever Fly. Palo Alto, Calif.: Klutz Press, 1998.
Blackburn, Ken, and Jeffrey Lamern. *Kid's Paper Airplane Book.* New York: Workman, 1996.

HIT THE DECK

Spend some time on the observation deck of your local airport if it has one. If not, just visit the airport and find a safe spot to watch the planes take off and land. Start a log of all the different types of airplanes you see. Observe how they appear in the sky as well as on the ground. Can you tell the difference between a helicopter and an airplane when it is a long way off in the sky?

Until you learn to identify different kinds of planes, you might want to take along a "field guide." Two good ones to try are:

Chaikin, Andrew L. *Air and Space: The National Space Museum Story of Flight.* Boston: Bulfinch Press, 1997.
Winkowski, Fred, and Frank Sullivan. *100 Planes 100 Years: The First Century of Aviation.* New York: Smithmark Books, 1998.

UP, UP AND AWAY

OK, so it's not exactly rocket science, but you've got to start somewhere. Get a simple helium-filled balloon (available at any party good store). Attach a small card with your name and mailing address. Ask whoever finds the balloon to write you and tell you where and when they found the balloon.

Take the balloon outside and let it go. Watch it as it gains altitude. Does it climb fast or slow? Does it go straight up or move away from you very fast? How does the weather affect its movement?

TAKE A RIDE

The Experimental Aircraft Association (EAA) has a program called Young Eagles that works to introduce kids to the wonder of flight. Find out if there is a chapter in your area. Many of them have a First Flight program that offers airplane rides to kids—with a few strings such as parental permission attached. Find details at their website at http://www.youngeagles.com.

FLY THE WEB

Who needs altitude when you've got the World Wide Web? A great place to find links to all kinds of information about flying, including organizations and games, is http://www.flybyweb.com.

You can also have fun at http://www.avanimation.com with their animated flying program. Don't forget to duck when the plane buzzes you!

CHECK IT OUT

Aircraft Owners and Pilots Association
421 Aviation Way
Frederick, Maryland 21701
http://www.aopa.com

Air Transport Association
1301 Pennsylvania Avenue NW, Suite 1100
Washington, D.C. 20004-1707
http://www.air-transport.org

American Institute of Aeronautics and Astronautics
1801 Alexander Bell Drive, Suite 500
Reston, Virginia 20191-4344
http://www.aiaa.org

Balloon Federation of America
P.O. Box 400
Indianola, Iowa 50125
http://www.bfa.net

Experimental Aircraft Association
P.O. Box 3086
Oshkosh, Wisconsin 54903-3086
http://www.eaa.org

International Organization of Women Pilots
7100 Terminal Drive, Box 965
Oklahoma City, Oklahoma 73159-0965
http://www.ninety-nines.org

National Aeronautic Association
1815 N. Fort Myer Drive, Suite 700
Arlington, Virginia 22209
http://www.NAA-USA.org

National Business Aviation Association, Inc.
1200 Eighteenth Street NW, Suite 400
Washington, D.C. 20036-2506
http://www.nbaa.org

Women in Aviation, International
Morningstar Airport

3647 S. R. 503 S.
West Alexandria, Ohio 45381
http://www.wiai.org

World Aeronautics Association
P.O. Box 390534
Mountain View, California 94039
http://www.meer.net

GET ACQUAINTED

Alan W. Neil, Airline Pilot

CAREER PATH

CHILDHOOD ASPIRATION:
Always wanted to be a pilot.

FIRST JOB: Working as a loading dock clerk for a Christmas tree manufacturing firm.

CURRENT JOB: Captain for American Airlines.

A MAN WITH A PLAN

As a pilot for one of the world's major commercial airlines, Alan Neil spends a lot of time getting ready to fly. Before he ever takes off in an airplane, Neil prepares himself mentally and physically for the trip. That involves several tasks. To keep himself in good physical shape, he runs several miles a day. His mental preparation centers around three major areas: knowing the basic systems of the airplane he's flying; reviewing the procedures to control those systems; and thinking about what he should do in case of an emergency.

He arrives at the airport early to give himself time to check on the airplane he'll be flying and to find out about any last-minute changes in procedures and airport information.

Weather along the route he will travel is scrutinized for "bumpy rides" and possible storms. In conjunction with the dispatcher, he plans the path the airplane will take and files the flight plan with the proper authorities.

When he gets to the airplane, he briefs the other pilots onboard (for international flights there must be relief pilots as well as those who are in the cockpit) and the flight attendants. He also takes time to meet the crew and walk through the plane. After all that, if everything is A-OK, he finally gets ready to take off.

SAFETY FIRST

There's no question that getting passengers safely to their destination is Neil's number-one priority. He says, "Passengers place their lives in my hands and I take that trust seriously."

That's why Neil checks out everything! He knows where to expect turbulence along the way and does his best to plan the route around it. "Sometimes," he says, "the coffee in the back goes flying when the plane hits an unexpected bump." With careful planning and some help from technology, that doesn't happen often.

Medical emergencies are handled with just as much care. One time a child became very ill on an overseas flight. While flight attendants on each flight are trained to take care of almost everything, they are not doctors. In this case, Neil and the attendants were directly in touch with a doctor on the ground. Neil had to be ready if needed to divert the airplane to a nearby airport for an emergency landing. Fortunately, the doctor was able to help, and the child was OK. The plane flew on to its destination.

TEAM EFFORT

Teamwork is what it takes to get a plane off the ground. However, the captain is ultimately responsible for everything that happens. Every team member has his or her job to do, and it is up to Neil to make sure their jobs get done right.

Team spirit is important to Neil, so he does his best to build camaraderie with the people he works with. While the airline provides meals only for passengers, it is not unusual for Neil to bring a pizza, his homemade sticky buns, or muffins for the crew. Christmas stockings stuffed with little goodies from Captain Santa have been known to appear on galley doors, too. Often the whole crew takes a sightseeing trip together when they reach their destination.

This attention to detail makes a difference. Neil takes pride in making sure that the plane is in top condition before take-off. Neil also enjoys walking through the plane (while another pilot is flying, of course!), talking with passengers, and making sure they are having a good flight.

A SKY-HIGH SMILE

Neil has been flying for many years. He always wanted to be a pilot, so when he graduated from college, he headed straight to the U.S. Air Force to become a fighter pilot. He later worked as an instructor for the air force, helping to train new pilots. Now he's a commercial pilot and flies mostly to Europe and the Caribbean. Imagine going to Paris or Puerto Rico once a week!

For Neil, the absolute best part of flying is the people. He flies all sorts of people, from rock stars to former presidents. But Neil says that there is nothing better than getting off an airplane, walking into the terminal, and seeing a child yell, "Grandma," with his or her arms open wide. Getting people together is what makes flying so special for him.

Astronaut

WHAT IS AN ASTRONAUT?

10, 9, 8 . . . Are you looking for career that's out of this world? 7, 6, 5, 4 . . . Have you ever wondered what it's like up there with the stars? 3, 2, 1 . . . Do you wonder what it would be like to be an astronaut and blast off into space? Astronauts (from the Greek words for "star sailor") are the men and women who explore the vast frontiers of outer space. They work to discover more about other planets, the Sun and Moon, and other galaxies. They investigate how and if life can exist in these different environments. Just like yesterday's cowboys explored the Wild West, today's astronauts explore the unknown reaches of the universe.

One of the most fascinating space projects now in the works involves creating an international space station that would allow astronauts from around the world to actually live on another planet. Astronauts living at this station will conduct experiments, explore other planets, and attempt to uncover many of the mysteries of outer space. Can you imagine someday sending a postcard from Mars to your friends on Earth? It could happen in your lifetime!

Currently, all U.S. astronauts work for the National Aeronautics and Space Administration (NASA). The biggest project now underway is the Space Transportation System,

28

also known as the space shuttle, which flies missions into orbits around Earth. Each mission includes a commander, or pilot, who is responsible for flying the spacecraft; payload specialists, who are responsible for conducting the scientific investigations and specialized activities contracted for by sponsors of the mission; and various mission specialists. Astronauts from other countries sometimes join the group, but a shuttle team is limited to eight people.

When shuttle astronauts go into space, they are launched into an orbit 115 to 250 miles above Earth where they travel more than 17,000 miles per hour and circle the globe every 90 minutes. That means they see the Sun rise or set every 45 minutes. By all accounts, it is a completely amazing experience!

Although astronauts play the most visible role in these missions, they would never get off Earth without the support of vast numbers of people on the ground. This support team includes aerospace engineers (who design, test, and build the systems and spacecraft), microgravity specialists, and mission control center experts. After the shuttle lands, other specialists and engineers inspect the shuttle for damage from its reentry into Earth's atmosphere and get it ready for the next flight. Teamwork is the key to making it all happen.

It isn't easy to become an astronaut. Although more than 4,000 people apply for these coveted positions, only 100 people are chosen every two years to go to NASA headquarters for interviews and extensive medical and psychological testing. Only 20 candidates make the final cut and actually go into astronaut training.

To qualify, you must meet vision and height minimums and have at least a bachelor's degree in engineering, science, or math plus three years of relevant experience. Most of those selected have advanced degrees in their field of expertise. Pilots usually are chosen from the ranks of the U.S. Air Force or another military branch. Good grades are a must, as is being in tip-top physical shape. Speaking more than one language is a plus. Not just anyone can withstand the pressures of being cooped up in a tiny spaceship thousands of miles from home, so NASA looks long and hard to find applicants who have the right stuff.

If you hope to get your shot at becoming an astronaut, you might as well start now by reading everything you can get your hands on about space, astronauts, rocket science, and NASA. Keep your grades up and stay in shape. Also, investigate some of the other occupations related to the space industry and see if you find other options for your talents and ambitions—just in case.

If you are one of the lucky ones who make the cut, you can expect to spend years training for what is likely to be just a few days or weeks in space. The first round of rigorous training lasts for a year and tends to weed out the wanna-bes from the real astronauts. Those who make it through that initial hurdle train constantly to learn new things about how equipment and systems work as well as how their bodies will function in space. They spend time experiencing zero gravity or working in a huge swimming pool practicing with their equipment while dressed in their bulky space suits. Before it's over, their training will have covered scuba diving, parachuting, land and sea survival training, shuttle systems, science, and technology. Tons of time is spent simulating all kinds of situations that could occur while they are in space. Every possibility and every stage of the launch are considered and practiced over and over again.

It's not easy, but it can certainly be exciting. Considering that space travel is a relatively new accomplishment, there is still much work to be done to discover the many wonders of the universe. Who knows what kinds of opportunities your generation will have to continue this incredible quest on behalf of humankind?

TRY IT OUT

COUCH POTATO ASTRONAUTS
Take a trip to space from the comfort of your couch after a visit to the local video store or library. Borrow copies of movies such as *The Right Stuff, Apollo 13,* or *From the Earth to the Moon* and get ready to blast off!

WALK A MILE IN THEIR SPACE SHOES
Read some of the fascinating stories of real-life space heroes in books like these:

Buchanan, Douglas. *Air and Space: Female Firsts in Their Field.* Bromall, Pa.: Chelsea House, 1999.

Hansen, Rosanna. *Astronauts Today.* New York: Random House, 1998.

Jones, Stanley P., and L. Octavia Tripp. *African American Astronauts.* Mankato, Minn.: Capstone Press, 1998.

Montgomery, Scott, and Timothy Gaffney. *Back in Orbit: John Glenn's Return to Space.* New York: Longstreet Press, 1998.

GERONIMO!
You don't have to be an astronaut to get some training from NASA. NASA has lots of space activities you can do on your

own or with some classmates. One fun idea is to make a parafoil (a parachute for spaceships). For more help go to http://quest.arc.nasa.gov/space/teachers/x38/. There you'll find a paper pattern, assembly instructions, and ideas for performance tests. You can compare it to a regular parachute, test it with different weights and under different wind conditions, and more.

You'll also find out-of-this-world fun and games at NASA's website at http://www.nasa.gov/kids.html. While you are at it, see what's up at NASA's Observatorium at http://learn.ivv. nasa.gov/features/1999/observe_feat/observe_feat.html.

A CYBERSPACE MISSION

More on-line space adventures are to be found at some of the following websites:

- http://school.discovery.com/schooladventures/ universe/index.html
- http://www.genastro.com/21stCentury.htm
- http://www-k12.atmos.washington.edu/k12/ resources/mars_data-information/mars_overview.html
- http://pds.jpl.nasa.gov/planets/welcome/mars.htm
- http://www.marsacademy.com/mt7.htm
- http://quest.arc.nasa.gov/space/background/index. html
- http://www.dfrc.nasa.gov/History/Publications/SP-4303/ch11-3. html, and watch the process from landing to launch at http://quest.arc.nasa.gov/space/ events/ ksc99
- http://liftoff.msfc.nasa.gov/academy/astronauts/ wannabe.html
- http://www.faahomepage.org/astronaut.html

SPACE VACATIONS

Can't wait to become an astronaut? Then you'd better start saving your pennies for a week at Space Camp. Space Camp has locations in Alabama, California, and Florida, and offers a variety of awesome astronaut training programs for kids from

the ages of 9 through 18. The program generally involves simulated space shuttle missions, training simulators (like the 1/6
gravity chair), rocket building and launching, and all kinds of
scientific experiments. For all the details, go on-line to
http://www.spacecamp.com.

CHECK IT OUT

Astronaut Hall of Fame
6225 Vectorspace Boulevard
Titusville, Florida 32780
http://www.astronauts.org/home.htm

EarthWatch Incorporated
1900 Pike Road
Longmont, Colorado 80501-6700

National Aeronautics and Space Administration
Lyndon B. Johnson Space Center
Houston, Texas 77058
http://www.nasa.gov

GET ACQUAINTED

Joan E. Higginbotham,
Astronaut

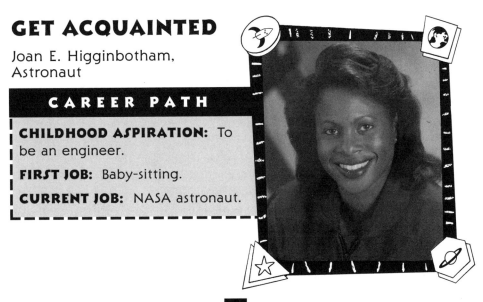

CAREER PATH

CHILDHOOD ASPIRATION: To
be an engineer.

FIRST JOB: Baby-sitting.

CURRENT JOB: NASA astronaut.

LOVE AT FIRST SIGHT

Joan Higginbotham went to college planning to be an electrical engineer. She'd even picked out the company she wanted to work for when she graduated—IBM—but it wasn't hiring when she was ready to start work. Then along came some recruiters from NASA. They made it sound like an interesting place to work, so Higginbotham took a trip to actually see the launch pad and the shuttle for herself. "It was like something out of *Star Wars.* I felt a keen sense of excitement just seeing it. That was when I decided I absolutely had to be an astronaut."

Her first assignment was to work on the team that launches the shuttle. While she was working, she earned master's degrees in management and space systems. Considering Higginbotham's experience and education, her friends thought she'd make a good astronaut and encouraged her to apply for the training program. She followed their advice, went through the interview process, and made it!

"This is an incredibly great place to work," Higginbotham says. "Women are given the same opportunities as the men, the same training, the same pay. It's a lot of hard work, and we're kept constantly busy." The only thing she sometimes regrets is not having more time to just relax.

NEVER A DULL MOMENT

Training is a big part of Higginbotham's job. One of her favorite training exercises involves experiencing the feeling of zero gravity. The exercise involves climbing steeply to high altitudes in a KC135 aircraft. At a certain point during the climb, there is a 20- to 25-second window of time in which she feels weightless. As the plane levels out and then descends sharply at the same angle as the climb, she floats. "It's an incredible feeling, and I love it," she says.

Astronaut training involves all kinds of challenging experiences. One day Higginbotham may find herself immersed in a huge tank of water dressed in her spacesuit, and putting together complex equipment. Another day she might be sitting in a simulator blasting off into "virtual" space.

Higginbotham explains that during these flight simulations, "they throw in every kind of failure they can think of to train us so we can anticipate, plan, and react effectively and efficiently."

Other training involves water survival, parachute jumping, scuba diving, and learning to flying a T-38 jet plane. "This was the hardest part for me—learning to fly at Mach One in the jet. It was such a new experience." Of course, working out every day (including weight and cardiovascular training) to keep in top physical condition is part of the job as well.

In addition to all this training, she works on learning Russian so she can function effectively with her international colleagues in the space station. She has also traveled to Russia (Moscow and Star City) to train with Russian cosmonauts, and was fascinated to observe both the similarities and the differences of life in another country.

OUT-OF-THIS-WORLD ADVICE

Higginbotham says that aspiring astronauts have to get great grades in school. Math and science skills are key in this profession, but so is getting a well-rounded education by taking all kinds of courses. Astronauts work as a team, so you have to work well with others—knowing when to lead and when to follow. You also need the self-confidence to get through any challenge and to be able to think fast in a constantly changing, dynamic environment.

If you want to be an astronaut, Higginbotham urges you to learn all you can about space as you finish school. She says it takes a lot of drive to get to work on the space shuttle. You have to really, really want it, and you have to work hard to get there. And getting there is just the beginning.

Carpenter

WHAT IS A CARPENTER?

Take a pile of fresh-cut wood and a handful of nails. Hammer a little here and sand a little there. What do you get? It depends. It could be a house, a wonderful piece of furniture, new kitchen cabinets, or even a sleek sailboat. Those are just a few things that skilled carpenters make using their own two hands, raw materials, and the tools of their trade.

Carpenters work on all kinds of projects that require wood as a main ingredient. It's highly skilled work that isn't as easy as it may look. Carpenters tend to specialize in a particular kind of work. There are framing carpenters who build the frames for houses and millwork carpenters who build doors, window casings, and trim. There are also shipbuilders and cabinetmakers. Some carpenters build new buildings or houses while others restore or renovate existing buildings. Highly skilled carpenters who have a penchant for history handle historic preservation projects. Some carpenters make a good living by helping people fix up or change their houses—perhaps by adding a new room or "finishing" a basement.

In addition to hammers and nails, carpenters may also use lathes, sanders, special saws (watch those fingers!), and other kinds of tools that are designed to do certain woodworking tasks. Carpenters often work according to very specific plans and must be exacting in their measurements to do their job right. "Just a little off" might as well be 10 feet off as far as the quality of the work goes. That's why strong basic math skills are essential for this kind of job. It's also why carpenters swear by the guiding rule "Measure twice and cut once."

Some carpenters learn the ropes at trade or vocational-technical schools. Many carpenters learn their trade on the job by working as an apprentice for someone with more experience. Formal apprenticeship programs are often offered by local chapters of organizations such as the United Brotherhood of Carpenters and Joiners of America, the Associated General Contractors, Inc., or the National Association of Home Builders.

There's really no substitute for "hands-on" learning in this line of work. You can only learn so much in books before you just have to get out there and do it.

A good carpenter knows to play it safe. The tools carpenters work with are not toys. If they aren't used properly, they can cause serious injuries. Many tools have safety features, and smart carpenters use them. They are also careful to use tools correctly and to wear proper safety gear such as hard hats, safety goggles, and steel-toed shoes.

Strong muscles are a benefit of this profession as the job is physically demanding. Lifting, climbing, and hammering are all part of a day's work—rain or shine.

Some carpenters move into construction management jobs where they plan and direct crews of workers from start to finish of a project. They must have a firm grasp of the rules, regulations, and building codes that apply to their area. These people spend most of their time scouting out new jobs, dealing with customers, and overseeing employees. Scheduling, coordinating, bidding, and estimating are all skills they need to do their job. They might be in charge of just their own crew, reporting to a general contractor, or they could perform the general contractor's duties and supervise the subcontractors. They are responsible for the safety of the workers on the team and the completion of the job within the time and budget constraints set down by the owner.

Carpenters usually start with a set of plans or blueprints that tell them exactly what to build. It takes skill and imagination to turn what they see on paper into a structure, a piece of furniture, or a piece of art. Some would say that one of the best parts of this job is the satisfaction a carpenter gets from making something out of nothing. Whether it's building houses or hospitals, crafting fine furniture, or constructing school desks for students like you, carpenters know that their work is a lot more than wood and nails.

TRY IT OUT

HOME SWEET HOME

Maybe you aren't quite ready to build your family's next home, but with a parent's help and permission, building a tree house might be the next best thing. For inspiration and instructions, visit these websites featuring kids who have built their own tree houses:

☀ http://gate.cruzio.com/seaweb/corbin/index.html
☀ http://www.btinternet.com/fulton.treehous.htm

If you can't find a tree large enough to hold the kind of tree house you want, build a small clubhouse on the ground instead. Paint the outside to protect the wood through all kinds of weather. Invite your friends over and have fun!

CARPENTERS AT WORK

If tree houses aren't your thing, never fear. There are more cool things for you to build. How about some yard art? Don't know what yard art is? Find out at http://www.accentsin-pine.com or http://btinternet.com/~fulton/treehous.htm.

If toys are your bag, check out these low-cost patterns for a fire truck, bulldozer, farm tractor, and other wooden toys at http://www.scrollsaw.com. Make one for a favorite little friend and they might think you are one of Santa's elves.

If you want to start with something nice and easy, go to your local hobby shop and take a look at their woodworking kits. These kits aren't free so you'll need to ask your parents to lend you a hand—and maybe a few bucks while they're at it.

TV TRAINING

Tune into your PBS and HGTV stations to find some interesting and informative television shows about building. Check local listings for shows such as *This Old House* and *Bob Vila's Home Again.* And speaking of Bob Vila, you'll find some pretty cool information at his website too—just go to http://www.bobvila.com.

HELPING HANDS

How does the idea of helping a family in need while learning how to build grab you? You can do that very thing by volunteering with a very worthy organization called Habitat for Humanity. Since 1976, this organization has built more than 85,000 simple, decent houses in their quest to eliminate housing poverty. Find out what you can do to help on-line at http://www.habitat.org or by writing to Habitat for Humanity, 115 E. 23rd Street, 10th Floor, New York, New York 10010.

CHECK IT OUT

American Council for
 Construction Education
1300 Hudson Lane, Suite 3
Monroe, Louisiana 71201-6054

American Furniture
 Manufacturing Association
P.O. Box HP-7
High Point, North Carolina 27261
http://www.afma4u.org

American Institute of
 Constructors
466 94th Avenue North
St. Petersburg, Florida 33702
http://www.aicnet.org

Associated Builders and
 Contractors
1300 North 17th Street
Rosslyn, Virginia 22200
http://abc.org

Associated General Contractors
 of America, Inc.
1957 E Street NW
Washington, D.C. 20006
http://www.agc.org

Construction Management
 Association of America
7918 Jones Branch Drive,
 Suite 540
McLean, Virginia 22102
http://www.cmaanet.org

United Brotherhood of|
 Carpenters and Joiners
 of America
101 Constitution Avenue NW
Washington, D.C. 20001
http://www.necarpenters.org

GET ACQUAINTED

Earl M. Walker Jr., Carpenter

CAREER PATH

CHILDHOOD ASPIRATION: To be a marine biologist or a professional athlete.

FIRST JOB: Washing dishes in his dad's restaurant.

CURRENT JOB: Craftsman specializing in making custom furniture.

OFF TO THE RACES

Earl Walker went to college to study marine biology and play basketball. While there, he got hooked on bicycle racing and spent the next 15 years racing professionally in the summer and going to college in the winter. Don't think the racing slowed down his education, though—he took so many college classes he earned 300 credits! That's more than twice the number he needed to graduate.

In addition, Walker's cycling took him all over the world and gave him the chance to do something he really loved. That's why, when he retired from racing, he knew his second career had to be something he'd enjoy. Since puttering around the wood shop with his grandfather making gifts for his mom and dad had always been a favorite pastime, he turned his attention to woodworking.

THEY SAID IT COULDN'T BE DONE

Walker and a friend bought an old wooden boat and spent hours fixing it up. They intended to use it for water-skiing and launched it with great expectations for a summer of fun. Unfortunately, it sank. So much for that idea.

So Walker moved on to other woodworking projects. Since he had some experience making furniture for friends all through college, he decided to start his own custom furniture business. Contrary to popular opinion, which says that furniture making isn't a good business to go into on your own, Walker has built a very successful venture. He's met every one of the goals he's set for the business, and he's having fun doing it.

THE GOOD, THE BAD, AND THE PAPERWORK

Walker loves to make furniture and work with wood. He hates paperwork. But guess what? Owning your own business and doing paperwork go hand in hand, so Walker gets stuck doing a lot of it. He says, "I spend a couple of hours each morning just doing paperwork. If I don't do a little each day, it gets really overwhelming and I can't face it. I'd rather be sanding a tabletop or choosing just the right piece of wood to use, not figuring out debits and credits and paying bills."

CRANKING UP THE CREATIVITY

To work with wood like Walker does takes a great deal of creativity. Walker has noticed that his creativity level has really grown since he started his business. He says, "I was always inventive, but this is more. Now creativity bursts out of me. I find myself grabbing a piece of paper during dinner so I can draw some new idea."

THERE'S MORE TO IT THAN MONEY

Making furniture is something Walker would do even if he didn't get paid—a sure sign that's he's doing something he loves. Working with wood is his passion. For him, it's exciting to see a piece come together. The thing he likes most about the process is seeing the smiles of his customers when he delivers the finished product. According to Walker, "They touch it, open the drawers and doors, smell the newness of it, and the look on their faces is the best payment of all."

ULTIMATE FREEDOM

So what do marine biology, bicycle racing, and carpentry all have in common? If you asked Walker, he'd say, "freedom." In each pursuit, Walker found the freedom to be resourceful and creative in his work. Walker would also say it's been quite an adventure!

Commercial Model

WHAT IS A COMMERCIAL MODEL?

You'll probably see the results of what commercial models do for a living before you go to sleep tonight. They are everywhere! Pass a billboard on the way home from school—there they are. Watch TV—there they are. Read the newspaper or flip through a magazine. Yep, they are there too. Commercial models are the people featured in commercials and advertisements to sell all kinds of products—not just clothes, either. Commercial models pitch everything from abalone to zwieback.

When you think model, the first thing that may come to mind is fashion model—those beautiful girls and guys who walk the runways for designers creating a glamorous image for the season's new fashions. To be a fashion model generally requires that you have a certain "look" and meet some pretty strict height and weight requirements. Some people think if you aren't drop-dead gorgeous, you'll never make it as a model, but that's not true. At least, not exactly. You may never grace the cover of the hottest fashion magazines unless you have the "look," but that doesn't mean there aren't other opportunities for people who look like—for lack of a better way of saying it—"real people."

Commercial modeling is part acting and part modeling. These models can be male or female, young or old, short or

tall, skinny or not so skinny. The job may require assuming a certain role such as a housewife going gaga over the new laundry detergent or a teen hip-hopping around in the latest cargo jeans for a television commercial. It may involve being photographed wearing fashions from a local department store for a newspaper ad. Some commercial models are known for special kinds of assignments such as hand modeling where the only thing photographed is their hands—usually wearing an exquisite piece of jewelry or advertising nail polish or another type of hand-care product.

There is no formal education required to be a commercial model. However, classes are often available through modeling agencies or finishing schools that provide training in some of the finer points of commercial modeling. Models are often represented by agents who scout out modeling assignments for them. Many models work in the industry only part time.

They may be full-time students or have another job that helps pay the bills and fill in off-camera time.

Models usually "market" themselves by putting together a group of pictures, called a composite, showing them in different settings and situations, wearing different types of clothes. Their composite is circulated among advertising agencies that evaluate it for the types of projects they are working on. If the model fits the criteria for a project, he or she could land an assignment. Other times models will go to an audition—a "go-see"—where Polaroid pictures are taken of the models in specific kinds of settings. This allows the photographer, the ad agency representatives, and the client to choose models that best meet the criteria they are looking for.

An actual photo shoot is full of action. Preparation may include makeup, clothes, hair styling, and rehearsal. All that comes before the camera starts rolling. After that it's not just a simple matter of smiling and saying "cheese." It can be hard work to get just the look the client is after. It can take dozens of poses and hundreds of shots.

After the shoot, there's still work to be done, mostly paperwork to be filled out: releases, contract vouchers, thank-you notes, invoices, and other items.

The work can be a bit glamorous at times, but mostly it's just hard work. It can get boring sitting around waiting for photographers to set up equipment and adjust lights. But it can also be lots of fun, involving travel to unusual places and providing a chance to make new friends.

One of the most important parts of being a model is staying true to your own goals, standards, and values. Sometimes it can be easy to get swept away in the excitement of it all. Commercial modeling isn't about being thin and beautiful or becoming a "star." It's about discovering the beauty that is already inside you and letting it shine. Be careful about falling for those "let me make you a star overnight" scams and always involve your parents in any modeling assignments you accept before you're 18. Set your sights on where you want to be and go for it!

TRY IT OUT

SAY CHEESE!

Save up your money for a couple rolls of film or a disposable camera (there are some nifty new versions). Get a friend or two together, some of your favorite outfits, and some interesting props. Take turns snapping photos of each other using a variety of emotions and going for different looks.

Use these photos to put together a composite. Mind you, this is just for practice. If you really decide to go after some commercial modeling assignments, you will need professional-quality photographs in your composite. However, this is a good way to get an idea of what the process is like.

SCOUT SOME TALENT

Turn the tables for this activity. Instead of being the model, take on the role of the agent or client. First, thumb through a magazine and pick a few products to sell. Maybe toothpaste, a sophisticated new perfume, a sports car, or a minivan. Cut out pictures of just the product and attach each one to a separate sheet of paper. Now go through the magazines again looking for photographs of the types of models who you think "match" each product. Think about what kind of model will sell each product best. Would it be a man or a woman? Should the model be old or young, short or tall, beautiful or ordinary? What kinds of clothes and props would help set the right mood? Clip any photos you like and attach them to the appropriate page. This will give you an idea of how models are selected for various projects.

BE CAREFUL OUT THERE!

Do not—repeat, do not—even consider a career as a commercial model until you read an article called "If You've Got the Look . . . Look Out!" found on-line at http://www.fashion.about.com/style/fashion/blmodel.htm. The article is courtesy of the U.S. Federal Trade Commission and provides some very frank cautions about the modeling industry. Read it and make two checklists: one for dos and one for don'ts. Make sure that your career decision is based on facts and good advice, not fantasy and scams.

MODELING 101

For a crash course in what it's like to be a model, assign yourself some homework in the following books:

Esch, Natasha. *The Wilhelmina Guide to Modeling.* New York: Fireside Books, 1996.

Matheson, Eve. *The Modeling Handbook: The Complete Guide to Breaking Into Local, Regional, and International Modeling.* New York: Henry Holt, 1995.

Preston, Karl. *Modelmania: The Working Model's Manual.* Marina Del Rey, Calif.: Dog Gone Books, 1998.

Rubenstein, Donna. *The Modeling Life: The One (And Only) Book That Gives You the Inside Story of What the Business Is Like and How You Can Make It.* New York: Perigee, 1998.

Williams, Roshumba. *The Complete Idiot's Guide to Being a Model.* New York: Macmillan, 1999.

Wilson, M. J. *A Model's Primer.* Brandon, Fla.: Advanced Multimedia Designs, 1997.

CYBER MODELS

Looking for the inside scoop on what it's like to be a model? You'll find tips, success stories, and all kinds of information at websites such as:

- ☼ http://www.supermodels.com
- ☼ http://www.modelsinfo.com
- ☼ http://www.webmodels.com

Find out how to look your personal best at websites such as:

- ☼ http://www.beautylink.com
- ☼ http://www.beauty.miningco.com/style/beauty/
- ☼ http://imagetools.com
- ☼ http://www.lookinggreat.com

CHECK IT OUT

Barbizon Agency and School of Manhattan
15 Pennsylvania Plaza
New York, New York 10001

Ford Models, Inc.
142 Greene Street
New York, New York 10012-3236

Ford Model Management
297 Newbury Street
Boston, Massachusetts 02115
http://www.candyford.com

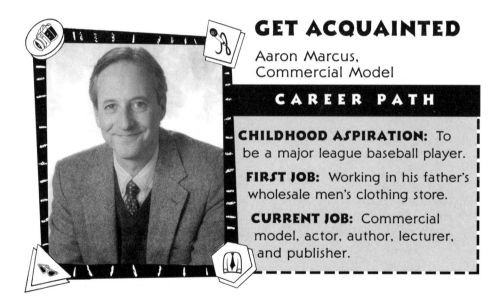

GET ACQUAINTED

Aaron Marcus,
Commercial Model

CAREER PATH

CHILDHOOD ASPIRATION: To be a major league baseball player.

FIRST JOB: Working in his father's wholesale men's clothing store.

CURRENT JOB: Commercial model, actor, author, lecturer, and publisher.

MUSICIAN TO MODEL

Aaron Marcus was a musician first and played in a band with his brother for six years. It was fun while it lasted, but he eventually opted out to go to school to become a physical therapist.

Once in school, however, he discovered a little problem. He needed to do something to support himself while he was going to school. He started to do a bit of commercial modeling just to pay the bills. He set some goals before he started, giving himself one year to earn enough money to finish his education.

As it turned out, Marcus really liked modeling. He liked it so much, in fact, that he decided to try it full time. He now earns enough in modeling to support his family of four.

A JOB YOU CAN GET INTO

According to Marcus, there's a special thrill of being on a job that's out of the ordinary. He finds that, especially when the emotional angle is tough, he has to totally immerse himself in the set, taking on the character he is supposed to represent. When he really gets into it, he's oblivious to anything else.

He spends time the night before getting ready and practicing, being sure that he has all the necessary props. He won't just show up and expect everything to go smoothly. Marcus spends a good chunk of time preparing, including getting that all-important good night's sleep.

"When everything goes well, when I'm totally prepared and am feeling all the right emotions, then the photographer and I get into a sort of dance—the rhythm of the shoot that makes everything just click." For Marcus, that's the best.

HO-HUM

Sometimes Marcus has to drive a very long distance to get to a shoot, which he doesn't mind too much. It's all the waiting on the set that can get to be a bit of a drag. To pass the time, he brings along a book to read while he's waiting. It could be a new novel, an acting book, marketing information about modeling, newsletters, or company magazines. He's learned never to go anywhere without something to read.

HELPFUL ADVICE

Marcus' advice to you is to do your homework before you start. He's had years of experience, thoroughly researched the modeling industry, and found there are a few things that are important to check out early. These include: getting photos done and putting together your composite, finding agents, making contacts, getting work on your own, getting the documents you need to have, and knowing when your parents should be involved. He advises that when you take a class, you should audit a couple of sessions first to see what it's like. It can save you in the long run. Marcus was so concerned that people would get hooked into stuff they shouldn't that he wrote a book about it. You can find out more it at his website at http://www.howtomodel.com or find out if your library has a copy of Marcus' book, *How to Become a Successful Commercial Model* (Baltimore: Marcus Institute of Commercial Modeling, 2000).

Computer Security Expert

SHORTCUTS

SKILL SET

✔ COMPUTERS

✔ MATH

✔ ADVENTURE

GO online to http://www.mysteries.com and see if you can crack the latest case.

READ *Cyber Crimes: Crime, Justice, and Punishment* by Gina DeAngelis (Broomall, Pa.: Chelsea House, 1999).

TRY creating your own secret code using the symbol keys on a computer keyboard.

WHAT IS A COMPUTER SECURITY EXPERT?

Viruses, cryptography (a method of protecting the content of messages), parasites, firewalls, and steganography. This word comes from Greek roots & literally means "covered message"; in the computer world it has to do with the concealment of messages. It's just another day on the job for a computer security expert. Instead of tracking down thieves and giving out traffic tickets, "cybercops" work to keep computer systems safe and secure.

One look around should remind you how important computers, the Internet, and other sophisticated technology have become in our world. Computers affect almost everything we do. From everyday visits to the gas station and grocery store to matters of international security, computers play a role in keeping our world on track and running smoothly.

Wonderful as all this progress has been, it hasn't come without its own set of problems. Computers, and especially worldwide Internet accessibility, have resulted in a new kind of crime. In its simplest form, it's called hacking. That's when someone with enough computer knowledge to cause trouble electronically "breaks into" someone else's computer system

and wreaks havoc. Sometimes it's meant to be a joke (except that it's not very funny); other times it's done with malice and an intent to disrupt things. In a way, hacking isn't much different from an unwanted intruder breaking into your house, going through all your personal stuff, and leaving a big mess.

Another common type of computer crime (and, yes, it is a crime) is writing programs called viruses and purposely spreading them through the computers of unsuspecting users everywhere. These bugs multiply fast as one computer user connects with another and so on down the line. The viruses lurk unnoticed in these computer systems until some pre-specified action "detonates" them—it could be simply turning on the computer, downloading information from the Internet, or opening a file. Kaboom! The damage is done, systems are down, and valuable information could be lost.

While the results of these viruses can spell bad news to personal computer users, it can be especially devastating to businesses and government agencies. Some reports estimate that the average cost to investigate, repair, and secure these big systems after a virus strikes can be more than 1 million dollars.

At the heart of all this are sensitive privacy issues. Whether it's your own computer or your bank's computer, it's sure to contain information that would best be left confidential. Much of the information would be difficult, if not impossible, to replace unless the user was savvy enough to take precautions.

Privacy isn't the only thing at stake here. Now that so many people, businesses, and governments depend on computers, a lot could go seriously wrong when someone starts messing around with their computers.

Here's where computer security experts, or cybercops, come into the picture. They use their computer skills to fight cybercrime and keep the world's computers safe. As you might imagine, hackers have to know more than a little bit about computers in order to do what they do. In order to track down these bad guys, cybercops have to stay a step ahead of them by keeping their computer skills sharp, current and creative.

If this is a field you'd like to consider for your future, plan on going to college and majoring in computer science. And, of course, it goes without saying that you might as well start now to learn your way around a computer.

Since there are two main ingredients in computer crimes—computers and criminals—you'll also need to learn a lot about people. In order to catch a hacker, you have to know how he or she thinks. Since a hacker could be sitting on the beach in Tahiti causing problems for a business in Australia, it can be especially difficult to find these crooks. One thing that a computer security expert does is create profiles of the perpetrators of these crimes. They look at age, sex, education level, hobbies, habits, and other factors to zero in on the troublemaker. To learn how to do this, cybercops need a good background in psychology and criminology in addition to their computer expertise.

Catching hackers is just half of a computer security expert's work. The other half is preventing computer crimes. That's where such things as firewalls, cryptography, steganography, and other kids of security measures come into the picture. Cybercops are often hired as consultants or employed by corporations or government agencies to design systems to keep their computers safe.

Whether the computer security expert is cracking crimes or preventing them, ethics plays a big part in this profession. Therefore, it helps if your own standards and values are above reproach.

As you begin to prepare for your own career, you can be certain that more advances in technology will bring more challenges for computer security. There is sure to be plenty of adventure waiting for computer security experts who are ready to do what it takes to crack the next case.

TRY IT OUT

BETWEEN A ROCK AND A HARD PLACE

Ethical dilemmas are just part of a day's work for computer security experts. These problems can be tricky because they often fall in the gray area between what is right and what is wrong. Can you think of any "iffy" situations where you weren't sure what to do? Following are a few simple situations to think about. Is there a right or a wrong answer?

- ☼ You put 50 cents in a soda machine and hit the jackpot! You not only get a soda, but you also get a handful of quarters as well. The machine has obviously malfunctioned. What's the ethical thing to do? Assume it's your lucky day and pocket the change, or report the problem and return the change to the owner of the machine?
- ☼ You told your mom you were going to the library. And you did intend to go to the library, but along the way you see some friends and end up going skateboarding

instead. When your mom asks how things went at the library, what do you say?

☼ You've been studying for weeks for an algebra test. Now the big day is here, and you are sweating it. The smartest kid in class is sitting in front of you, and if you tilt your head just right, you can see her answers without the teacher noticing what you are doing. What do you do?

Sometimes the ethical thing to do is not the easiest thing to do. To figure out some ethical solutions for these situations and any you encounter on your own, take this little ethics quiz and see how your answers measure up.

☼ Am I doing the right thing?
☼ Could I justify my actions if I get caught?
☼ Am I willing to accept the consequences for taking this action?
☼ If someone did this to me, would I like it?
☼ Will I feel good or guilty about this action tomorrow?
☼ Would I be proud or embarrassed if all my friends and my parents knew about this?

CYBERCIPHER

Try your hand at solving this cipher puzzle. This is a simple substitution problem. Solve it and see what it says. (Hint: Q equals C.)

QAPZENIO KLOEBIB MOI RANCLRS NA BRIIXI MN. BNAZ NCIP DIGAOI NCIH QMR BZOIMF.*

Look for other puzzles, especially math puzzles, you can solve. Keep your curiosity sharp. By the way, the answer to this puzzle can be found at the end of this chapter.

TRUTH AND CONSEQUENCES

Remember all the concern about computers crashing for Y2K? Fortunately, disaster did not strike as some had predicted. But what if the world's systems did go down for a day or two? How would your life be affected?

Get a blank sheet of paper and draw a little stick figure in the middle of the page. That's you. Now make a chart diagramming all the ways that your life would change without computers. Don't limit yourself to things that you do on your own computer. Think about all the ways that computers touch your life and add those to your list too.

CYBERCOP STUFF

Computers are the weapon of choice for cybercops everywhere. Make sure your skills are in peak condition by learning all you can. Following is a potpourri of websites that may interest a future computer security expert.

- ☼ Find out your ethics "style" at http://www.ethicsandbusiness.org/stylequiz.htm.
- ☼ Ponder the ethics case of the month at http://www.engr.washington.edu/~uw-epp/Pepl/Ethics/ethics2.html.
- ☼ What does a hacker look like? Find out what the experts say about that and other cyber security issues at http://www.wildlist.org.
- ☼ What is that "cookie" doing in your computer? Find out at http://www.cookiecentral.com.
- ☼ Hone your thinking skills and have some fun figuring out the brainteasers at http://www.cyberkids.com.

CHECK IT OUT

Americans for Computer Privacy
1275 Pennsylvania Avenue NW, 10th Floor
Washington, DC 20004
http://www.computerprivacy.org

Center for Democracy & Technology
1634 I Street NW, Suite 1100
Washington, DC 20006
http://www.cdt.org

Computer Security Institute
600 Harrison Street
San Francisco, California 94107
http://www.gocsi.com

Corporate Network Associates, Inc.
3965 Freedom Circle
Santa Clara, California 95054
http://www.nai.com

Electronic Privacy Information Center
666 Pennsylvania Avenue SE, Suite 301
Washington, D.C. 20003
http://epic.org

Lawrence Livermore National Laboratory
7000 East Avenue
Livermore, California 56741
http://www.llnl.gov

The Society for Electronic Access (SEA)
P.O. Box 7081
New York, New York 10116-7081
http://www.sea.org

GET ACQUAINTED

Sarah Gordon,
Computer Security Expert

CAREER PATH

CHILDHOOD ASPIRATION: To be a paleontologist.

FIRST JOB: Making and selling nylon sponges door-to-door.

CURRENT JOB: Data security analyst.

DINOSAURS AND VIRUSES

As a young girl, Sarah Gordon was fascinated by dinosaurs, so much so that she was planning to be a paleontologist until a teacher told her that she couldn't because she was a woman. Of course, the teacher was wrong, but Gordon didn't realize that at the time. She abandoned her dream and went on to other things, later becoming interested in computers and the Internet.

Gordon found her niche in computer security almost by accident. She had purchased a computer, discovered it had a virus, and became intrigued with how and why it had gotten there. So Gordon started digging to find out more and ended up doing so much research that she began writing papers on the results. It didn't take long before some of her work attracted the attention of some big companies and organizations, and they invited her to speak at meetings and conferences all around the world.

Now Gordon has a thriving business fixing viruses, testing clients' systems for security flaws, and working with the IBM Research Group to help develop and test technology to detect and remove new virus strains.

TOOLS OF THE TRADE

Gordon uses several computers to do her work. She keeps the computers that do the virus analysis totally separate from the ones she uses to test products. Her e-mail and research go on another computer. All viruses and potential viruses are essentially isolated so that she can study them without "infecting" the other computers.

AROUND THE WORLD

Gordon has discovered that her work has opened up the world to her—virtually and in reality. At first, she just spent lots of time talking with people from other countries on-line. As her business grew and she started to do more speaking, she found herself actually traveling all over the world to such places as South Africa, England, and Central America. Now she is recognized as an international authority on computer viruses and ethics.

According to Gordon, the best trip she's taken was to Greece. She says, "I spoke at a conference on a tiny little Greek island. The water was crystal clear, the people were so friendly, and it was like something out of a movie. I absolutely loved it."

FROM THE PATIO

Telecommuting is another perk of the job. That means Gordon can work wherever she wants to and finds that she enjoys working from home even though it takes a great deal of self-discipline. Sometimes her work is tough to put away at night. Gordon admits that she "can get so absorbed in what I'm doing that I almost forget where I am."

MAKING THE WORLD A SAFER PLACE

Gordon's commitment to making the world a safer place to work and play keeps her going in this job. She explains that, "At times it's boring sitting there tracing codes and analyzing programs for viruses, but I never know what I'll find next. There's always something new right around the corner: a new virus, a new twist on things, a different hacker with a new tool trying to get into a client's system. I do everything I can to wipe out this junk."

* Cybercipher Solution: Computer viruses are nothing to sneeze at. Stop them before they spread.

Detective

SKILL SET

✔ TALKING

✔ COMPUTERS

✔ ADVENTURE

GO find out if your local police station offers tours or special programs for young people.

READ a good mystery and see if you can figure out who committed the crime.

TRY deciphering the hidden message with the Secret Code Kit. Find one at a local toy store or order one on-line from http://www.etoys.com.

WHAT IS A DETECTIVE?

Whether it's a murder or a lost child, a bank robbery or insurance fraud, a terrorist threat or business espionage, tax evasion or contraband drugs, you can bet that there's a detective on the case. The law boils down to this—crime does not pay. It is a detective's job to track down the culprits and bring them to justice.

There are lots of different kinds of detectives including police officers working in small rural communities, private investigators, and special agents for the Federal Bureau of Investigation (FBI). Police detectives may work to solve a specific type of crime such as homicide. Highway police officers often must investigate the causes of automobile accidents and other incidents. Fire departments have special investigators who determine the cause of fires. This type of work is usually assigned to experienced police officers with special training.

The federal government also employs several different kinds of detectives. Most widely known is the FBI. These agents may investigate terrorism, bank robberies, organized crime, and kidnappings, and then will often work in cooperation with local law enforcement agencies to solve a case. Other government detectives include Immigration and

Naturalization Service agents, U.S. marshals, and special agents for the Bureau of Alcohol, Tobacco, and Firearms (ATF), the Internal Revenue Service, the Secret Service, and U.S. Border Patrol.

Private investigators work on a large variety of cases for individuals or corporations. These cases may be centered around corporate espionage, shoplifting prevention, electronic surveillance, finding family members, or other kinds of problems involving families. Another type of private investigator, a bail bondsman, or bounty hunter, will help to find those people who have skipped bail and bring them in to stand trial. Often, a corporation will employ a full-time security expert, another type of detective, to be sure the company's ideas, employees, and products are safe.

Along with detectives who work the streets solving crimes through investigations, interrogations, and other methods, there are detectives who work in laboratories looking for clues in some of the most unusual places. They include the doctors, called coroners, who perform autopsies as they look for clues about how a person died. Also included are the forensic scientists or criminologists who look for clues in the evidence gathered by detectives. They use such things as fingerprints, fiber analysis, and DNA tests in their work. Another kind of detective is a profiler, who specializes in the psychological side of things, studying criminal behavior and giving other detectives ideas about the kinds of people capable of committing certain types of crimes.

For all of these people, the work can be dangerous, time-consuming, and extremely stressful. A detective never knows what a new day will bring and must be ready for anything. Detective work seldom involves gunfights and high-speed car chases like you see on TV. Instead there is a lot of careful, routine work that involves gathering clues, sifting through evidence, talking to people, checking out computer information, searching through records in courthouses and libraries, and testing and retesting theories and ideas. It might mean sitting on surveillance detail for long periods of time just watching and waiting for someone to do something. Paperwork, and lots of it, is another part of the job.

Detective work requires training and experience. Sometimes, as in many police departments, experience counts as much as or more than education, so detectives often rise through the ranks of the department. Other kinds of detective work, especially those involving the federal government and those involving complicated scientific skills, do require college degrees. For instance, if you want to work for the FBI you must have a college degree plus a law or accounting degree, or you must have work or language experience to compensate. All jobs generally require some on-the-job training as well, which can range from a few weeks to a few months. Passing written and practical tests is also necessary to become licensed.

Detective work can be an ideal choice for the adventurous type with a strong sense of right and wrong. Curiosity, good people skills, and creative and analytical thinking skills also come in handy in this line of work.

TRY IT OUT

WHICH WAY DID IT GO?

Can you solve the mystery of the missing money? Have several friends gather in a room. You leave the room and ask your friends to secretly choose one person to be the "thief." Place four quarters in a bowl in the center of the table. Turn off the lights and count to 10 while the thief steals the coins.

Come back into the room and investigate the crime. Ask questions. Listen carefully. Can you figure out who did it?

PRINT YOUR FRIENDS

You can purchase a fingerprint kit in most toy stores or on-line at http://www.etoys.com. Use it to fingerprint some of your friends or family members. Notice the differences between each person's prints.

Now leave the room. Have one friend pick up a glass while you are away. Come back and try to determine the "culprit."

For some fingerprinting tips, go to the FBI's kids' page at http://www.fbi.gov/kids/crimedet/finger/fingerpt.htm.

THE CASE OF THE MISSING BOOK

Here's a case that's sure to need your detective skills. Ask your school librarian if there are any books that have mysteriously disappeared. If your school is like most, there will be a few. Try using your detective skills to track it down. Who had it last? Do they still have it? Where was it last seen? Can you get it back?

ARMCHAIR DETECTIVES

There's nothing quite like a good mystery story. Along with some great classics such as the Hardy Boys mysteries and Nancy Drew adventures, there are now some fun ways to solve the crimes on-line. Look for clues at websites such as:

- http://www.kidsloveamystery.com
- http://www.TheCase.com/Kids
- http://www.MysteryNet.com
- http://www.NancyDrew.com

ON-LINE INVESTIGATIONS

Here are just a few websites of interest to young detectives. Do some investigating on your own and you're sure to find more.

☼ Listen to the detective tips at http://www.hitekinfo.com/snoop/audiosafive.htm.
☼ Check out the ATF's kids page at http://www.atf.treas.gov/kids/resources.htm.
☼ Find out why secret service agents wear sunglasses at http://www.treas.gov/usss/kids.htm.

CHECK IT OUT

Bureau of Alcohol, Tobacco
   and Firearms
650 Massachusetts Avenue NW
Washington, D.C. 20226
http://www.atf.treas.gov

Federal Bureau of Investigation
   J. Edgar Hoover Building
935 Pennsylvania Avenue NW
Washington, D.C. 20535-0001
http://www.fbi.gov

National Association of
   Investigators and Adjusters
101 West 6th Street, Suite 330
Austin, Texas 78701
http://www.naia.com

National Council of Investigation
   and Security Services
1730 M Street NW, Suite 200
Washington, D.C. 20036
http://www.nciss.com

United States Border Patrol
Immigration and
   Naturalization Service
Border Patrol Special
   Examining Unit
425 I Street NW
Washington, D.C. 20536
http://honorfirst.com

United States Border Patrol
   Supervisor's Association
539 Telegraph Canyon Road,
   P.M.B. #656
Chula Vista, California
   91910-6497
http://www.bpsups.org

United States Department of
   Justice
Drug Enforcement
   Administration
Information Services
   Section (CPI)
700 Army Navy Drive
Arlington, Virginia 22202
http://www.usdoj.gov/dea

United States Marshals Service
Employment and
   Compensation Division
Field Staffing Branch
600 Army Navy Drive
Arlington, Virginia 22202

United States Secret Service
Personnel Division
1800 G Street NW, Room 912
Washington, D.C. 20223
http://www.treas.gov/usss

GET ACQUAINTED

Paula Washow,
Private Investigator

CAREER PATH

CHILDHOOD ASPIRATION: To be a secretary.

FIRST JOB: Baby-sitting.

CURRENT JOB: Director of her own private investigating firm.

A LONG HAUL

Paula Washow started her career as a legal secretary when her two children were small. The job was a long way from her home, and it limited her time with her kids. When a friend told her about a job with a nearby private investigator (PI), she grabbed it.

After a while, she started getting suspicious of the detective she was working for, so she gave him notice that she was quitting. Before she had a chance to quit, the sheriff's office, the FBI, and some bill collectors showed up looking for her boss. Forget the notice—Washow was out of there!

A BETTER WAY

Washow's first foray into the world of private investigators didn't turn out so well. However, that didn't stop her when a friend suggested that she partner up with someone who wanted to start a PI firm. This time she decided to do it right.

More than 25 years later, Washow is in charge of a well-regarded PI firm. Her company provides executive protection, electronic security, and background investigations, among other things. This time, she's the boss, and she sets the standards high and runs the business right.

HAPPY ENDINGS

One of the most rewarding things Washow does is help families discover lost relatives, find missing children, and contact biological parents or children. It's nice to share in the joy of bringing people together.

Sometimes the stories don't end so happily. Washow says that the hardest part of her job is to work hard to find someone only to find out they have died. It's tough to break the bad news to the client.

WHAT A BORE!

As much as Washow enjoys her job, there are some things she has to do that are just plain boring. Surveillance is one of them. All she does is wait and watch. Sometimes it means sitting in a car on a cold, snowy night, watching the front door of a building for someone to enter or leave. Sometimes she must wait in the corner of a hotel lobby for someone to check in or watch a restaurant for two people to meet. She can't even read a book because she has to have all her senses tuned in to what's happening around her. It's tedious—but a necessary part of the job.

PERSISTENCE PAYS

Washow says that this business requires the tenacity of a pit bull. In order to complete an investigation, you have to uncover every clue you can find. Then go back and find a few more. Look at a problem from several different angles. Listen with your whole body and all of your senses. Be able to listen to conversations around you, even when you're talking to someone else. When someone tells you "it can't be done," you've got to find a way to do it.

A PI IN THE WORKS

If you want to become an investigator someday. Washow advises you to get a college degree in criminal justice or police science. Learn all you can about human behavior and investigation tactics. Don't get discouraged. The preparation will make you a much better detective in the long run.

Expedition Leader

SHORTCUTS

SKILL SET

✔ ADVENTURE

✔ ANIMALS & NATURE

✔ SPORTS

GO lead a group of friends on a nature hike.

READ *The Lewis and Clark Expedition* by Patrick McGrath (Parsippany, N.J.: Silver Burdett Press, 1996).

TRY climbing an indoor climbing wall at a recreation center near you.

WHAT IS AN EXPEDITION LEADER?

This career is all about discovery—discovery of new places, new people, and new experiences. Some expeditions involve physical daring—a trip to Nepal to climb Mount Everest, a scenic bike tour to see the leaves in New England, sea kayaking in Baja, or a challenging hike through a national park. Others involve special interests such fashion, art, or history. People go on expeditions to take on new challenges, discover new worlds, or learn something they didn't know about themselves.

The leader of an expedition is responsible for pretty much everything that makes an expedition so exciting. Managing the basics like travel arrangements, food, and lodging are one part of the job. Another part is planning a schedule of events that will provide a memorable experience for each customer. The expedition leader must carefully attend to every detail. Routes and transportation must be exact, activities must be planned, arrangements must be made, employees must be trained, food and supplies must be sufficient, equipment must be in good repair, emergency supplies must be on hand, and so on. In cases where expeditions are held off the beaten path, such as a jungle safari or white-water rafting trip, there won't be a convenience store or fast food restaurants on every corner. (There might not even be a corner!)

What you carry in your backpack is what you've got to survive on, so good planning pays off.

Generally speaking, an expedition leader must be physically fit. If backcountry skiing is the purpose of the expedition, the leader must be an awfully good skier. The same thing goes for scuba diving, fishing, whatever the type of the expedition. Expedition leaders have to know their stuff.

Quite often, physical rigor isn't the only focus of expeditions. Many revolve around learning about a wide range of topics. Whether it's antiques or marine biology, team members expect the leader to be an expert in the field—or close to it.

People skills are a must to lead and motivate all kinds of people through all kinds of challenging situations. Problem-solving skills won't hurt, either, since there are always new situations to work out.

There really isn't a "school" that you can attend to become an expedition leader. People drawn into this profession usually do so because of a passion for a certain activity or place. In one sense, they are teachers, using the world as their classroom. In another, they are true adventurers, stretching the limits of themselves and others.

TRY IT OUT

BACKYARD TREK

You don't have to go far for an expedition. Take a couple of friends on a trek to your own backyard. Get your parents' permission and gather supplies to camp out overnight. You'll need food, shelter, a source of light, and so on. Make sure to plan a full schedule of challenging events. Put together an obstacle course, schedule some "Olympic-style" competitive events and any other activities you think your friends would enjoy—safely. Maybe some scientific experiments or stargazing would fit the bill. Don't forget the ghost stories!

If you find yourself in need of ideas for fun activities, take your pick from those described in these books:

Carlson, Laurie, and Judith Dammel. *Kids Camp!: Activities for the Backyard or Wilderness.* Chicago: Chicago Review Press, 1995.

Drake, Jane. *The Kids' Summer Handbook.* New York: Ticknor and Fields, 1994.

TOPS THIS IF YOU CAN

While the theme of expeditions can vary greatly, all expeditions have one thing in common: adventure. Find out about some of the most adventurous expeditions on record (so far!) in books such as these:

Baker, Nancy. *Explorers and Discovers: From Alexander the Great to Sally Ride.* Farmington Hills, Mich.: Gale Group, 1999.

Engelbert, Phyllis. *Explorers and Discoveries.* Farmington Hills, Mich.: Gale Group, 1998.

MacDonald, Fiona. *Explorers: Expeditions and Pioneers.* Danbury, Conn.: Franklin Watts, 1994.

For more information about the famous adventures of others, go to the library or go on-line and do a search for "explorers." Who knows? We may be reading about one of your adventures someday!

LOST AND FOUND

Here's an activity that's sure to build your courage and confidence. Ask an experienced adult to take you on a trek in the woods. Pack your backpack with some snacks, some water, a trail map, and a compass. Take a look at the map and decide where you want to go, and then tuck the map away in your backpack. See if you can rely on the compass for directions and your wits for guidance to get you where you want to go. Look at the map only if you must to keep from getting lost.

JOIN THE CLUB

If it's adventure you are looking for, you don't have to look far to find it. Your local chapter of the Boy Scouts or Girl Scouts offers all kinds of opportunities for challenges and fun. For more information about these organizations, go on-line to http://www.girlscouts.org for Girl Scouts and http://www.bsa.scouting.org for Boy Scouts.

WEB ADVENTURES

You don't have to worry about bugs when you take an on-line expedition. Try some of these websites and let your imagination run wild. What would it be like to really be there?

Find out what the Earthwatch Institute is doing in the areas of research, education, and conservation. See how you can volunteer to help at http://www.earthwatch.org.

Take an expedition on-line at http://www.expeditionresearch.org.

Take a trip to the bottom of Monterey Bay or go to some other exotic place on the globe when you travel with National Geographic at http://nationalgeographic.com.

TAKE YOUR PICK

There's something for everyone at a website called the Summer Opportunities Channel. Here you'll find a database of every imaginable kind of summer camp program and academic and travel adventure. Sports nuts, photography buffs, fashion plates—you name it and they list it.

You can also find the same information in book format. *Peterson's Summer Opportunities for Kids and Teenagers* is published each year by Peterson's Guides and is widely available in bookstores and libraries.

CHECK IT OUT

African Safari Company
P.O. Box 4337
Seattle, Washington 98104
http://www.africansafarico.com

Amazonia Expeditions
10305 Riverburn Drive
Tampa, Florida 33647
http://www.perujungle.com

Earthwatch Institute
Three Clocktower Place
Suite 100, Box 75
Maynard, Massachusetts 01754
http://www.expeditionresearch.org

National Geographic Society
1145 Seventeenth Street NW
Washington, D.C. 20036-4688
http://www.nationalgeographic.com

Tsanza Adventures, Inc.
815 Cherry Avenue
Eugene, Oregon 97404
http://www.amazonrainforest.com

Tusker Trail and Safari Company
6800 Owensmouth Avenue, Suite 310-A
Canoga Park, California 91303
http://www.tusker.com

Williwaw Adventures
Wilderness and Sailing Expeditions
P.O. Box 166
Kingston, Massachusetts 02364
http://www.williwawadventures.com

GET ACQUAINTED

Martha Culp,
Expedition Leader

CAREER PATH

CHILDHOOD ASPIRATION: To be a veterinarian.

FIRST JOB: Baby-sitting and weeding people's yards.

CURRENT JOB: President and director of Inside Out, Inc., which provides adventure expeditions for kids.

INQUIRING MIND

When Martha Culp was growing up, she loved being out-doors. She enjoyed hiking, camping, and splashing in streams. As a child, she often collected water samples at nearby streams and ponds. Then she'd go home to look at things under her microscope.

Now that she's an adult, her company, Inside Out, Inc., is a natural fit. She gets to work with kids, which she loves, and her work involves one adventure after another. She plans expeditions that go all over the world. It's an incredible job! You can find out more at Culp's website at http://www.insideout-inc.com.

CHALLENGE BY CHOICE

One thing Culp tries to do with each expedition is provide opportunities for kids to make challenging choices and to develop new skills. The idea is to gently nudge them to accomplish things they never thought they could do. Whether it's rock climbing or rushing down a river in a kayak, kids break through their own barriers at their own speed. Depending on the situation, this part of Culp's job can either be really fun or really hard.

Sometimes it's tough to stay quiet when students are trying to figure out how to overcome a challenge. The easy way out would be for Culp to just tell them what to do, but that would defeat the entire purpose of the challenge. She's learned to bide her time and watch for each person to find their own solutions to problems.

CHART THE COURSE

Planning and more planning is what Culp does before each trip. Logistics is a big deal when you are trying to get a group of people and a bunch of equipment from one place to another. Food, equipment, and other supplies must all be packed ahead of time.

Every piece of gear must be inspected to make sure it's in working order. Tents have to be tight, sleeping bags clean and rolled, and ropes ready. "There's nothing worse than waking up in the middle of the night with rain dripping on your face because there's a small hole in the tent," Culp says. Her job is to make sure that doesn't happen.

SAFETY IN NUMBERS

Safety is also a big concern for Culp. Teamwork is one way that Culp makes sure that her expeditions are as safe as possible. For instance, when rock climbing, one person climbs a sheer wall of rock, while another secures the rope that keeps the climber safe. Each team member must be able to trust the others to do their part.

Culp says that a while ago she took an expedition into the woods with a group of kids who had never been camping before. They didn't know how to pitch a tent or build a fire or cook their food. No one knew anyone else, so communication didn't come easily. On the expedition, the group began to learn new things together. They really jelled as a team and began to interact with each other. Culp says, "By the end of the trip, they really didn't need me. It was fun to watch the different personalities come together to do the jobs that needed to be done."

NEVER A DULL MOMENT

This job is full of diverse and interesting things to do. There isn't a typical day or a typical program or a typical group. It's all different. Culp finds herself morphing from one area to the next as she works out logistics, checks gear, orders food, sets up activities, and figures out van points and campsites.

"There's nothing boring about this job," she says. "Each moment is filled with a discovery of some new thing in the universe, a new way of doing things, a personal limit that is pushed. I challenge myself, whether it's working on gear maintenance, taking a long hike, or doing the office work. That's part of discovering more about me."

Firefighter

SKILL SET

✓ SPORTS

✓ ADVENTURE

✓ MATH

GO visit a nearby fire station.

READ *A Firefighter* by Stephanie Maze (Chatham, N.Y.: Raintree/Steck-Vaughn Publishers, 2000).

TRY running up and down several flights of stairs, wearing a backpack full of books.

WHAT IS A FIREFIGHTER?

Thank goodness for firefighters! If you've ever been in a fire, an accident, or other emergency, you know what how important their work is. Sirens wailing and lights flashing, firefighters will be there when bad things happen.

Whether it's a fire, an accident, a medical emergency, or some other type of catastrophe, firefighters are trained to handle almost any situation that comes their way. The training starts with several months of intensive firefighting preparation and it really never stops. As long as people keep finding new ways to get into trouble, firefighters need to keep learning ways to help them.

Before the training starts, however, potential firefighters have to meet some fairly rigorous requirements, including passing a written test, a physical test of strength and endurance, and a medical examination. Applicants must be at least 18 years old and have a high school education or equivalent. A college degree isn't required, but those who have a college degree or have taken some community college courses in fire science have a better chance of being hired. Often competition is heavy for the few firefighter slots available.

Physical fitness is critical to performing well in an emergency. Fires aren't easy to fight. Before the flames die down, a firefighter may have to handle large hoses that carry heavily

pressurized water, run up flights of stairs, climb ladders, and rescue people or pets. Even though those tasks are hard enough all by themselves, firefighters must do them while wearing heavy protective gear and equipment.

Fighting fires isn't the only thing that firefighters do. Hazardous materials, floods, earthquakes, terrorism, medical emergencies, and accidents also get the trucks rolling from the firehouse. In addition, firefighters are often called upon to rescue people and animals that need help—including cats stuck in trees.

Day or night, when the call comes, firefighters answer immediately. That's why firefighters generally work in 24-hour shifts and sometimes sleep at the fire station at least a couple of nights a week. But if the alarm rings at 3 A.M., it is up and at 'em. If it rings at dinnertime, dinner has to wait.

Some firefighters also visit schools and provide programs on safety and fire prevention. They perform inspections on older buildings and work with builders to make sure that plans for new structures comply with fire codes. They may also work in conjunction with law enforcement officers to protect both people and property.

Other firefighters, called "hot shots" and smoke jumpers, work with the U.S. Forest Service to prevent and put out forest fires as well as rescue hikers and climbers. Sometimes you'll see stories about their heroic efforts on TV during the hot summer months when forest fires often rage out of control.

Fires at refineries, gas stations, chemical plants, or paint stores are especially dangerous and require firefighters with special training and equipment. In these cases, a hazardous materials truck goes out on the call, staffed by firefighters who have special training in that area.

Any kind of firefighting is dangerous work. That's why firefighters take safety very seriously. Injuries can occur from smoke inhalation, floors collapsing, explosive gases and chemicals, and other dangers. Good training not only helps firefighters do their job, but it also keeps them safe. Many times it can mean the difference between life and death.

Firefighting isn't a way to get rich quick by any means. But sometimes being a hero is worth a lot more than money. If you've ever been rescued by one, you know that *hero* is the only word that adequately describes a firefighter.

TRY IT OUT

HOME, SAFE HOME
Pick up a home inspection checklist from your local fire station or go on-line to http://www.pp.okstate.edu/ehs/links/fire.htm for links to all kinds of fire safety information.

Use the checklist to inspect your own home for fire safety. How do you rate? Be sure to test your smoke alarms. Locate all the exits in your house. In a fire, would you be able to get out in time? Pick a place away from the house for everyone to meet in case of a fire. Hold a fire drill for your family.

ON-LINE FIREFIGHTING
You can learn a lot on-line about fighting fires and preventing them. Here are a few websites to try:

- ☼ Can you survive alive? Find out in this simulated fire situation at http://www.survivealive.org.
- ☼ Fire safety activities can be found at http://www3.sympatico.ca/amills/HOMEHT~1.HTM.
- ☼ Listen to live broadcasts of fire station dispatch calls in your choice of cities at http://www.netnowonline.com/scanner/#real.
- ☼ Find out more about smoke jumpers at http:// www.smokejumpers.com and at http://www.nwlink.com/~rhubble/smokejumpers/what.htm.
- ☼ Visit a website where real firefighters go for the latest information at http://www.firefighting.org.

TELL THE SAFETY STORY

Get together with a couple of your friends and write a skit on fire safety for little kids. You'll find tips from the pros at http://www.justforlafs.org. This organization teaches firefighters how to use clowns, puppets, skits, and other memorable formats to teach children about fire safety. Can you come up with a hit skit? Ask your teacher to help you find a way to present your program to other kids in your school or a nearby preschool.

FIRE FIGHTING BY THE BOOK

Books are another interesting way to find out more about what it's like to be a firefighter. Following are some ideas to get you reading about a future fighting fires:

Camenson, Blythe. *Firefighting.* Lincolnwood, Ill.: NTC Publishing Group, 1995.

Conway, W. Fred. *Firefighting Lore: Strange but True Stories from Firefighting History.* New Albany, N.Y.: Fire Buff House, 1994.

Gorrell, Gena K. *Catching Fire: The Story of Firefighting.* Plattsburgh, N.Y.: Tundra Books, 1999.

Maze, Stephanie. *I Want to Be a Firefighter.* New York: Harcourt Brace, 1999.

Paul, Caroline. *Fighting Fire.* New York: St. Martin's Press, 1998.

CHECK IT OUT

International Association of Firefighters
1750 New York Avenue NW
Washington, DC 20006
http://www.iaff.org

National Fire Academy
16825 South Seton Avenue
Emmitsburg, Maryland 21727

National Fire Protection Association
One Batterymarch Park
Quincy, Massachusetts 02269
http://www.nfpa.org

United States Fire Administration
16825 South Seton Avenue
Emmitsburg, Maryland 21727

GET ACQUAINTED

Tracee Kelly, Firefighter

CAREER PATH

CHILDHOOD ASPIRATION: To be a teacher.

FIRST JOB: Baby-sitting.

CURRENT JOB: Firefighter and paramedic.

FROM ALASKA TO ARIZONA

Tracee Kelly grew up in Alaska and wanted to be a teacher. But she remembers being fascinated by the firefighters who came to her school to talk about safety. However, she assumed it wasn't a job for a woman.

By the time she graduated from high school, she was all set to go after a career in medicine. She went all the way through college and earned a pre-med degree.

Then she took some time off from school to work as a "hot shot" firefighter for the forest service in Arizona, and she loved it. Kelly ended up spending two summers digging fire breaks and helping to contain forest fires. She hiked with other hot shots and camped out, doing work that was very challenging physically. Great meals, along with the opportunity to make new friends and learn about fires, almost made up for not being able to shower and having to sleep on the ground.

THE BOOT

The experience in Arizona changed Kelly's life. She decided to use what medical training she already had as a firefighter instead of going on to become a doctor. She was accepted into a firefighter academy where she went through fire fighting "boot camp," a challenging training experience. Even now on the job, she must continue to get 30 hours of additional training each month in areas of firefighting, emergency medical procedures, and hazardous materials.

Kelly also spends at least an hour a day, when she is on duty and off, working out. "All of us are very athletic," she says. "I have pull my weight here. That means being able to pull hose, carry heavy packs, and run up stairs quickly." Being in shape can mean the difference between life and death in some situations. She keeps fit so she never lets the rest of her team down.

FIREHOUSE FAMILY

Firefighters often become an extended family. During 24-hour shifts, Kelly and four firefighters work, live, eat, and relax together. They take turns with such things as meal preparation and cleanup. "The neat thing is," Kelly says, "if you cook, you don't have to clean up." Dinners especially are lively, with lots of teasing, and occasional harmless pranks on one another.

Just like real families, when the going gets tough, this family sticks together. If one member becomes injured or sick for a long period of time, it's not unusual for others to cover extra shifts so he or she doesn't miss a paycheck.

Firefighters often help with on-the-job problems and personal ones as well. "We're there for each other, just as a family would be," she says. "We truly are our brother's keeper, both on the job and off. We depend upon each other, especially when people's lives are at stake. We have to function as a team, a family, in order to get things done."

LOTS OF LAUGHS

Firefighting boots and hat isn't the only uniform that Kelly wears. Quite often, she also wears a clown costume and goes to schools with other firefighters to talk about fire safety. As a clown, she can reach the younger kids with important, life-saving information, and have a roaring good time while she's at it.

MORE THAN WORTH IT

For Kelly, the most exciting part of her job is being able to help others. She tries to stay very aware of the fact that, when firefighters are called, it is often because of bad news. People are scared and in danger. Sometimes she is able to help turn tragedy into triumph.

Knowing her work can make the difference gives Kelly the courage to do what she needs to do. Every time she hears the bell in the fire station, jumps into her gear, and takes off on a fire truck with sirens wailing and lights flashing, Kelly knows she is on her way to save lives.

Military Serviceperson

SKILL SET

✔ ADVENTURE

✔ TRAVEL

✔ SPORTS

GO visit your local military recruiter.

READ about the history of some of America's greatest battles from the Revolutionary War to the Gulf War.

TRY running farther or faster than you have ever run before.

WHAT IS A MILITARY SERVICEPERSON?

Preserve, protect, and defend—that's what military servicepeople are charged to do each day. In the United States, there are four basic military branches, each with a different and vital role to play. The army serves on land with ground troops and tanks, the navy serves in ships that roam the world's oceans, the air force serves in planes and jets in the air, and the marines help with support forces on land, in the air, and at sea. Two supplementary services also lend a hand to keep our country safe—the Coast Guard protects our coastal waterways, and the National Guard provides military support in times of crisis.

You may be amazed to discover how many choices you'll have if you opt for a career in the military. With more than 700 military specialties available and more than 500 civilian support occupations, there are lots of ways for you to "be all that you can be." Some people make a career out of military service and devote 20 or 30 years of their lives to it. Others join the military to train for a career they want to pursue outside the military. It's a great way to gain excellent skills and work experience, develop your leadership ability, and earn benefits toward a college education.

Military jobs include front-line combat positions as well as electronic-related jobs in communications and intelligence, health care, administrative support, skilled trades such as carpenters and plumbers, and positions in service and supply. There are also highly technical positions in meteorology, surveying, and mapping as well as more "creative" ones in photography and music.

Military personnel are divided into two separate categories: officers and enlisted personnel. Officers are the military's leaders. They start out as first lieutenants with the cream of the crop ultimately earning the status of general. Personnel in either category gain rank and increased responsibilities and pay through exemplary performance and time in service.

Currently about 15,000 officers are commissioned into the military each year. Officers must have a college degree. Many receive their degrees and military training from a military academy such as West Point, the Naval Academy, or the Air Force Academy. Competition to enter one of the academies can be keen. To enter, you need to meet all the basic requirements, plus be no more than 23 years old, be unmarried with no dependents, have excellent grades and test scores, and be nominated by a member of the U.S. Congress. The Coast Guard Academy does not require congressional nomination, but accepts students on a competitive basis.

Joining the Reserve Officers' Training Corps (ROTC) is another way to become a military officer. This program works with students at certain colleges around the country, providing military training during the school semesters and requiring full summers of military service. ROTC students receive college scholarships in exchange for serving on active duty for a certain number of years after they graduate from college.

In addition to officers, there are about 190,000 enlisted people recruited into the military each year. To enlist in any branch of the service, you must have a high school diploma or its equivalent and meet vision, height, weight, and overall health minimums. In addition, you must be over the age of 17, be a U.S. citizen or permanent resident, and pass a written test.

Whether officer or enlisted, everyone goes through 6 to 11 weeks of basic training ("boot camp") plus additional training in their specialty area. Depending upon which occupation you choose, you could spend more than a year in initial training. Often the training is rigorous, and seemingly impossible at first. Some of it is designed to test your mental and physical limits, and it can be a real growing-up experience.

All military branches are open to both men and women. Only a few front-line combat jobs are limited to men; otherwise the opportunity, requirements, and standards are equal for all.

Serving in the military is different from working a civilian job. It's not just a job; it's a lifestyle. Most bases and ships are like cities unto themselves. Whether for a few years or for a lifetime, it can be a great way to see the world and serve your country.

TRY IT OUT

BOOT CAMP

Do you have what it takes to make it through boot camp? You might be surprised. One way to find is to get together with a few friends and stage your own boot camp. Plan several challenging activities such as a physical fitness test, an obstacle course at a local playground, and maybe even a map-reading activity. Be careful but push yourselves a bit to find out how tough you really are.

Or next time your school offers the Presidential Physical Fitness Test, get yourself in shape to pass every event. Practice, practice, practice—that's what it always takes to succeed.

GET OFF THE COUCH!

The military is no place for a couch potato, so get up and get yourself in shape. Check in with your physical education instructor at school and design a program of running, sit-ups, and aerobic exercises that will get you in tip-top shape. Find an indoor climbing wall to help you with your climbing and rope skills. Consider entering running or biking marathons in your area. Keep it up, and you'll be ready for anything!

WINNING WAYS

Winning a war is all about strategy, often with mind winning over muscle. You can get an idea of the strategy behind a military battle with a bucket of toy plastic soldiers, horses or tanks, and airplanes. (If you are interested in a naval battle, be sure to pick up the ships you need.) You can find these in most toy stores.

But first, spend some time in the library. Find out all you can about a battle fought during the Civil War, World War I, or World War II. How many soldiers were on the field and in what positions? Place your soldiers as they may have been during the battle. Now, re-create it in front of you. What strategies were used? If something had happened different-ly, would it have changed the way the battle went?

VIRTUAL MILITARY

Each of the military branches has its own website. Check out the army at http://www.army.mil. You can find the marines at http://www.usmc.mil.

The navy has a great site at http://www.navy.mil. Check out its kids' page with games and activities at http://www.navyjobs.com, and find out about the Blue Angels at http://

www.blueangels.navy.mil. Take the SEAL challenge at http://www.sealchallenge.navy.mil.

Get in on the action with the Stealth Force and find out about the air force experience at http://www.airforce.com or http://www.af.mil.

Another option is the U.S. Coast Guard. Find out all about this branch of the service at http://www.uscg.mil.

The National Guard provides many opportunities for both full-time and part-time service. Its web address is http://www.ngb.dtic.mil.

JUNIOR ROTC

Many high schools offer junior ROTC programs that provide military training for teens. Find out if your high school has a program and plan to join. It's a great way to find out if the military life is a good choice for you—and to find out how you look in a uniform!

READ ALL ABOUT IT

Before you sign up for military service, make sure you have all the facts. It's not a decision to be made on a whim. Once you sign, you're in and there is no getting out until your time is up. For more information about opportunities available in the military, look through books such as these:

America's Top Military Careers: The Official Guide to Occupations in the Armed Forces. Indianapolis, Ind.: JIST Publications, 2000.

Hutton, Donald B. *Guide to Military Careers: Air Force, Army, Coast Guard, Marines, Navy.* Hauppauge, N.Y.: Barron's Education Series, 1998.

Paradis, Adrian A. *Opportunities in Military Careers.* Lincolnwood, Ill.: VGM Career Horizons, 1999.

CHECK IT OUT

Your best source of information is your local army, air force, navy, marine, coast guard, or national guard recruiter. Look for their addresses and phone numbers in your local telephone book.

United States Air Force
   Academy
Colorado Springs, Colorado
   80840-5025
http://www.usafa.af.mil

United States Coast Guard
   Academy
15 Mohegan Avenue
New London, Connecticut
   06320-4195
http://www.cga.edu

United States Military
   Academy
West Point, New York 10996
http://www.usma.army.mil

United States Naval Academy
Leahy Hall
117 Decatur Avenue
Annapolis, Maryland
   21402-5018
http://www.nadn.navy.mil

GET ACQUAINTED

Cary R. Cooley,
Military Serviceperson

CAREER PATH

CHILDHOOD ASPIRATION: To be a pilot.

FIRST JOB: Mowing lawns.

CURRENT JOB: U. S. Navy SEAL.

ONCE IS ENOUGH

Cary Cooley played soccer in high school and hoped to go to college on a soccer scholarship, but after he was in a car accident, he needed to find a new plan, he started looking into the military. Nothing seemed like quite the right fit until he met a U.S. Navy SEAL.

The work sounded fun and appealed to his competitive spirit from soccer, his love of teamwork, and his willingness to work hard. All this was put to good use when Cooley went through Basic Underwater Demolition/ SEAL (BUD/S) training.

"The BUD/S training is the toughest the military can throw at you. If you can make it through that BUD/S training, you can do anything," he says. "You're wet and cold, tired and hungry. You get only four hours of sleep in more than five days of grueling training. Constantly being pushed, you're face deep in mud, sand, and ocean most of the time. You discover your body can do things you never thought it could do, and your mind can pull on reserves of energy you didn't know existed. I found out that the only easy day was yesterday." Only 15 percent of BUD/S candidates make it all the way through. It's that tough.

For Cooley, it may have started out as something cool to try, but it ended up taking sheer grit just to complete the training. Having survived the initial training, he went on to discover a career he loved.

MUD, GLORIOUS MUD

Since then, Cooley has been happily slogging through conditions most of us would rather not know about. He's camped out in the desert, the jungle, the forests, and the mountains, often going for weeks at a time without bed or bath. This is not your typical nine-to-five job, which is one of the reasons Cooley chose it.

"One time, our mission was to check the underside of a ship for bombs. The water was so gross, they wouldn't let us in until we'd had special shots to combat the bacteria." It's a tough job—good thing there are people like Cooley willing to do it!

MOVE, SHOOT, COMMUNICATE

Part of the Navy Special Warfare Command, the elite SEALs are the eyes and ears of the conventional military forces. They gather intelligence, do special reconnaissance jobs, ambush, sabotage, and infiltrate. These men are the kings of stealth, moving silently in the night, seeking out their targets.

Since most of the earth is accessible by water, they become especially adept at moving through the oceans and rivers on their way to a target. Sometimes SEALs come into an assignment area by submarine, by boat, or by parachute. Other times, a helicopter swoops down on a drop site, hovering for a few brief seconds while a platoon of SEALs "fast-ropes" to the ground.

MAN OF STEEL

You won't hear many people accusing SEALs of being wimps. It's physically demanding work, and the only way to handle it is to stay strong and healthy. SEALs, Cooley among them, have been known to run 14 miles and swim 5 1/2 miles using the side stroke or breast stroke. "It's a great job," he claims. "They pay you to work out!"

FROM HOT TO COLD

Cooley's work has taken him all over the world. He's tramped through freezing ice and snow 500 miles north of the Arctic Circle, and he's climbed the mountains and hills of Korea (he speaks both German and Korean fluently).

On one maneuver, his team camped in a remote North American desert. They had no food or supplies and had to exist on whatever they could find. Cooley discovered barbecued rattlesnake isn't so bad when you're hungry.

DESERT STORM TEAMWORK

Supporting main force units during Operation Desert Storm in the Persian Gulf War was probably Cooley's proudest moment as a Navy Seal. "It was amazing to see how all the branches of the military worked together to support each other's efforts. We got terrific help. Everyone was motivated to be there, and we all worked hard toward a common goal. It was really exciting."

Miner

SHORTCUTS

SKILL SET

✔ MATH
✔ SCIENCE
✔ ADVENTURE

GO back in time and join a virtual gold rush at http://www.museumca.org/goldrush.

READ Ian Wallace's *Boy of the Deeps*. (New York: DK Publishing, 1999).

TRY starting your own rock collection.

WHAT IS A MINER?

Go west, young man! It was the rallying cry of the gold rush during the mid-1800s. Hoping to strike it rich, gold miners scoured the hills west of the Mississippi River all the way to the Pacific coast. For the miners, it was backbreaking work, often done in damp, hard places where the sun never shines.

Fortunately, as mining activity expanded to include exploration for other minerals and resources such as silver, ore, copper, nickel, zinc, lime, and coal, so did the technology to harvest the materials. Tools and equipment powered by electricity and compressed air have revolutionized the industry. It's still hard work, mind you. But in many ways it's easier now than it was back in the 1800s.

Miners work in underground or open pit mines. In order to harvest the earth's treasures, they use drilling and hauling equipment and handle explosives and blasting procedures. Miners are also responsible for keeping mines safe by reinforcing drifts, walls, and other surfaces, and for transporting the ore through the drifts.

There are many types of mining jobs, and each one is very specific. Some miners install the bolts that support the roof of a mine, some operate the machines that extract raw resources from the mine, and others split large blocks of stone in a quarry. A pit truck driver drives the trucks that transport the quarried product out of the mines. Other miners work as pump operators and explosive experts (blasters).

All of these jobs require special training. To qualify for jobs like these, you must have a high school education. In some cases, special training in a particular area of expertise is also required. Some jobs require certification as well. However, in many cases, the best training is provided on the job.

Most miners work regular eight-hour shifts. Unions and mine owners work together to ensure that the workers have conditions that are safe and fair. However, the conditions in which a miner works can still be difficult and hazardous, especially in underground mines. Many of the more modern mines are air-conditioned, with cafeterias and break rooms provided, but some mines are not so well equipped. Cave-ins, while not as common as they were 100 years ago, still happen, so mines are carefully shored up as they are dug. All around, safety is extremely important.

There are other types of jobs associated with mining as well. Some are highly technical and require at least a bachelor's degree from college. For instance, mining engineers design the mines and plan the mining operations. They use their knowledge of rock mechanics, soils, mechanics, transportation systems, and machinery to keep mines running as

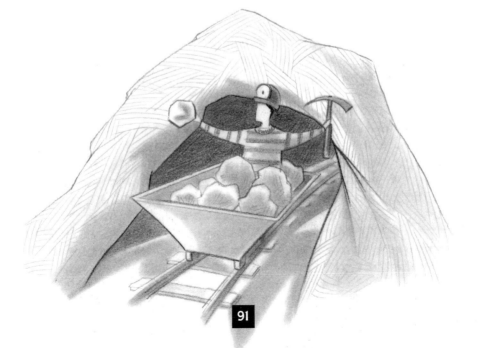

efficiently and productively as possible. Mineralogists and geologists are rock scientists who often consult with mining operators about the various aspects of the project. In addition, metallurgists supervise the extraction of metals from their ores using heating processes called pyrometallurgy, solution processes called hydrometallurgy, and electric processes called electrometallurgy to eliminate the impurities.

Environmental concerns also play an important role in modern mining operations. It is no longer standard operating procedure to strip a mine dry and then take off for another site. Miners are sensitive to maintaining the environmental integrity of an area and many take care to protect the land and plant life that surround the mine.

Mining is a profession that is forever linked with the heritage of our country. It provides valuable resources that enrich our lives. The work is challenging, the workplace unique, and the rewards can be satisfying.

TRY IT OUT

HONK IF YOU LIKE ROCKS

There is a bumper sticker around that says "It all comes back to mining." Most often found on the bumper of a miner's car, it means that many of the products we use and the resources we depend on everyday are linked in some way to mining. Is this true? Find out for yourself with this fairly simple activity. First, set up a chart with several columns. At the top of each column write the name of a natural resource found by miners. For instance, in one column you could write *ore*, in another write *gold*, in another write *nickel*, and so on. Now start digging around and find out what kinds of products are made from each of these minerals and list them in the correct column. To find out, go to the library and look at books on mining and minerals, ask your parents and teachers, and just snoop around.

HIT THE JACKPOT!

To get a better idea of mining opportunities and an appreciation for the size of this industry in America, go on-line to visit these mining career websites. See which jobs interest you the most and notice what kind of training and experience they require.

- ☼ Careermine at http://www.infomine.com
- ☼ The Mining Employment Page at http://www.miningusa.com

GHOST TOWNS

Mining is a profession with a past. It enjoys a rich history full of tall tales and fascinating stories. Go back in time and find out all you can about mining in days gone by. Your library is sure to have some good books on the subject and you can also find a "gold mine" of information at websites such as:

- ☼ The Mining History Network at http://www.ex.ac.uk/~Rburt/MinHistNet/
- ☼ The Mining History Association at http://www.lib.mtu.edu/mha/mha.htm
- ☼ American Mining History Links at http://www.rootsquest.com/~amhisnet/topic/mine.html

DIGGING FOR GOLD

There are many other websites of interest to potential miners.

Get the coal facts at http://www.wvcoal.com. Find out what "met coal" and a shuffle car are.

Find out where all the mining museums are located at http://www.msha.gov/TRAINING/MUSEUM/MUSEUM.htm.

Check out the kids' library at http://kids.library.wisc.edu.

Do you know why mines can be dangerous places? Check this out at http://www.msha.gov/KIDS/DANGER.htm.

CHECK IT OUT

American Coal Ash Association
2760 Eisenhower Avenue, Suite 304
Alexandria, Virginia 22314

American Institute of Minerals Appraisers
5757 Central Avenue, Suite D
Boulder, Colorado 80301

American Institute of Mining
P.O. Box 625002
Littleton, Colorado 80162-5002
http://www.smenet.org

American Institute of Mining, Metallurgical and Petroleum
    Engineers
Three Park Avenue, 17th Floor
New York, New York 10016-5998

American Institute of Professional Geologists
7828 Vance Drive, Suite 103
Arvada, Colorado 80003

Geological Society of America
P.O. Box 9140
Boulder, Colorado 80301
http://www.geosociety.org

The Gold Institute
1112 Sixteenth Street NW, Suite 240
Washington, D.C. 20036

International Precious Metals Institute
4400 Bayou Boulevard, Suite 18
Pensacola, Florida 32503-1908

Mineral Economics and Management Society
P.O. Box 721
Houghton, Michigan 49931

Mineral Information Institute
501 Violet Street
Golden, Colorado 80401
http://www.mii.org

Mine Safety and Health Administration
4015 Wilson Boulevard
Arlington, Virginia 22203
http://www.msha.gov

National Mining Association
1130 Seventeenth Street NW
Washington, D.C. 20036
http://www.nma.org

The Office of Surface Mining
United States Department of Interior
1951 Constitution Avenue NW
Washington, D.C. 20240
http://www.osmre.gov

Women in Mining
1801 Broadway, Suite 760
Denver, Colorado 80202

GET ACQUAINTED

Kadri Dagdelen, Miner

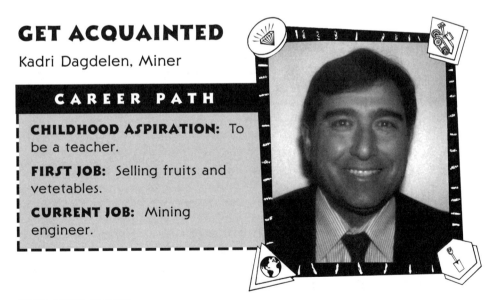

CAREER PATH

CHILDHOOD ASPIRATION: To be a teacher.

FIRST JOB: Selling fruits and vetetables.

CURRENT JOB: Mining engineer.

IT'S THE DIRT

Kadri Dagdelen grew up on his father's farm in the hills of Turkey. As a boy, he enjoyed working hard, running the farm equipment, and getting dirty. He remembers being at school one day and seeing a picture in a book of some American miners. "They were on a beautiful Rocky Mountain hillside, wearing blue jeans and boots and looking at rocks. They looked so fresh and happy, I thought I wanted to do the same," Dagdelen explains.

A WORLD OF MINES

Dagdelen's work has taken him around the world. He has visited and designed mines in the United States, South America, Canada, Australia, Central America, Europe, and central Asia. He even spent time in Russia evaluating copper mines. An interesting benefit to his work in mines has been the opportunity to meet people from many different cultures.

WORKING ON THE EDGE

Dagdelen spends most of his time working on special projects for different mines. He plays close attention to how to extract the earth's minerals without damaging the environment. "When we close a mine, we try to restore the area to its original condition. It isn't always possible, but we are always thinking about the impact on water, land, and plants."

Dagdelen's other big concern is safety. A current project involves using computers, satellites, and wireless telecommunications devices installed in mine trucks to keep drivers from driving off the edge of the waste material dumps. "When operating a truck as tall as a three-story building, the drivers can't see where they are. If we can devise a computer screen that will show them where they are, we hope to save many lives."

IT'S A BLAST!

For Dagdelen, riding down into the mine on a shaky elevator, not knowing what you will find at the bottom of the shaft, is exciting. "You don't know what to expect. Water drips down on you from above, the cage trembles as it descends into the dark, and the anticipation builds. It's like being on a roller coaster, except you know what to expect on a roller coaster. You don't in a mine."

It's this thrill of discovery that makes this job so adventurous.

Oil Rig Worker

SHORTCUTS

GO visit a gas station and compare the different grades of gas. Keep track of the prices and see how often they go up and down over several weeks.

READ *Opportunities in Petroleum Careers* by Gretchen Dewailly Krueger (Lincolnwood, Ill.: VGM Career Horizons, 1998).

TRY making a list of all the things we use oil and gas for.

WHAT IS AN OIL RIG WORKER?

Oil is an essential resource in modern life. People all over the world depend upon it for energy. Oil is used in materials as diverse as fertilizer, plastics, paint, and medicine as well as gasoline, jet fuel, and heating oil. Quite frankly, the modern world could not function without oil. Until someone comes up with a better source of energy, oil is essential. So, companies and governments invest lots of money and resources to get it.

This need for oil leads to a wide variety of opportunities in the oil and gas industry. There are opportunities for scientists such as geologists and petroleum engineers as well as opportunities for businesspeople who run oil companies and merchants who own gas stations. Perhaps one of the most adventurous career options in the oil and gas industry is that of an oil rig worker.

Drilling for oil is a risky and very expensive operation. Oil is found beneath the surface of the earth. Many times, oil wells have to be drilled very deep to reach the crude oil. Quite often, oil wells are drilled from oil rigs standing on the ocean floor. Many oil rigs are located in the ocean and must reach several thousand feet below the surface to reach solid ground, which means they aren't located right along the shore where oil rig workers can spend their lunch hours on the beach. Oil rigs tend to be way out where the only signs of life are in the water.

There are two types of oil rigs: those that drill for oil and those that pump oil to pipelines or tankers, which transport the oil to refineries. As you might imagine, there are many different kinds of skills needed to keep an oil rig functioning properly. In fact, since the workers generally live on offshore rigs for extended periods of time, there are usually opportunities for many positions, from cooks and galley hands to supervisors and engineers.

On a drilling rig, the manager of the rig is called a tool pusher. It's the manager's job to determine how far to drill, when to cap the well, when to move the equipment, and when to pack it up. He or she is totally in charge and needs special training to know how to make such important decisions. The driller, or shift boss, supervises a shift of workers and reports to the tool pusher.

The mudman mixes a special blend of mud used to cool the drill bit and move the rock cuttings from the hole back to the surface. Large tanks on the surface hold mixed and recirculated mud, so a mudman may mix at one site and then move on to another site to mix a new batch. This too requires some very specific training, much of which can be learned on the job over time.

Other workers on a rig include derrick hands, drivers, roughnecks (the ones who do heavy work), lease hands (responsible for helping the roughnecks keep the rig clean), and roustabouts (general laborers). Drilling oil also requires lots of additional help from surveyors, well consultants, truckers, water haulers, caterers, bit and mud suppliers, welders, corers, and loggers. There are also people who work on site preparation and clean up after a rig leaves.

Offshore rigs also need scuba divers and remote operated vehicle (ROV) operators. ROVs are tethered robots that are programmed to descend to extreme depths, perform mechanical functions, and report back to the surface—things that would be impossible for people to do. Based upon complex engineering procedural commands, they can assemble equipment several thousand feet down. They also inspect pipelines for damage and rig structures for wear and tear. An ROV operator controls the robot from the surface while sitting on a rig or a construction barge.

Most rig work requires special training beyond a high school education. In many cases, on-the-job training is the best way to prepare for the work. College is required for positions in engineering, geological consulting, or oil and gas surveying.

Working on an oil rig is hard physical work. Rig workers have to contend with all kinds of weather, from tropical, hot, and humid rainy conditions to frigid snow and sleet in the Arctic Circle and North Sea. The work can also require long stints of time far away from home—and far away from anything else, for that matter. Schedules can be unusual, ranging from 28 days work with 28 days off to 7 days work with 7 days off. These difficult schedules explain why the pay for any kind of work on an oil rig tends to be high. Some say you can expect a minimum of $1,000 per week for an entry-level position. With training and experience, the pay goes higher.

Work on an oil rig is, no doubt, an adventure. It's challenging and quite unlike a typical office job. The work can take you around the world and expand your horizons in ways you've never imagined.

TRY IT OUT

JOURNEY TO THE CENTER OF THE EARTH

Take a trip to the center of the earth. For a simple (and wacky) introduction to earth science, start with the *Magic School Bus: Inside the Earth* by Joanna Cole (New York: Scholastic Trade, 1989). An interesting on-line resource called *Oil on My Shoes* can be found at http://abix.com/oil. Once you get a handle on some of the basics, go to other resources and see what you can find out. For instance, which layer of the earth is most likely to have oil in it?

DRILLING THE DEPTHS OF THE WEB

You may be relieved to find out that the middle of the deep blue sea isn't the only place to find out more about oil rigs. Just click on some of these Internet sites and let them take you all over the world.

First stop is Caracas, Venezuela, for some late-breaking news and trends at http://www.gasandoil.com/goc/company/.

Move on to a refinery in Africa and find out how a refinery works at http://www.mbendi.co.za/.

Learn what the petroleum industry is all about at http://www.ems.psu.edu/~radovic/petroleum.html.

Don't miss your chance to take a virtual tour of an authentic offshore drilling rig at http://www.rigmuseum.com. If you are lucky enough to live nearby, you can actually walk aboard the famous "Mr. Charlie" oil rig at the International Petroleum Museum and Exposition in Morgan City, Louisiana.

Last stop, get answers to some of your nagging questions about oil. For instance, what does the "weight" mean on a can of motor oil? Find out at http://www.howstuffworks. com/question164.htm. And find out something you've always wanted to know—the differences among gasoline, kerosene, diesel fuel, and crude oil—at http://www.howstuffworks.com/ question105.htm.

A LITTLE OIL CHAT
If you have any intention of heading out to an oil rig some- where, make sure you know the language of oil. Go on-line to http://www.coloradousa.com/glossary.htm to find oil-specific definitions for words like these:

- Blow-out
- Christmas tree
- Fishing
- Kick
- Mud
- Topsides

MORE CAREERS IN OIL
For information about other careers related to the oil and gas industries, take a look at a book by Gretchen Dewailly Krueger called *Opportunities in Petroleum Careers* (Lincolnwood, Ill.: VGM Career Horizons, 1998).

You can also learn a lot about opportunities in the industry from some of the biggest petroleum producers around. Go on-line to visit:

- Arco at http://www.arco.com
- BP Amoco at http://www.bpamoco.com
- Chevron at http://www.chevron.com
- Exxon Mobil at http://www.exxon.com

CHECK IT OUT

American Association of
Drilling Engineers
P.O. Box 214332
Dallas, Texas 75221-4332

American Association of
Petroleum Geologists
1444 South Boulder Avenue
P.O. Box 979
Tulsa, Oklahoma 74101
http://www.aapg.org

American Association of
Professional Landmen
4100 Fossil Creek Boulevard
Fort Worth, Texas 76137-2791
http://www.landman.org

American Gas Association
1515 Wilson Boulevard
Arlington, Virginia
22209-2402
http://www.aga.com

American Institute of Mining,
Metallurgical and Petroleum
Engineers (AIME)
345 East 47th Street
New York, New York 10017
http://www.idis.com/aime

American Petroleum Institute
1220 L Street NW
Washington, D.C.
20005-4070
http://www.api.org

Association for Women
Geoscientists
P.O. Box 280
Broomfield, Colorado 80038-0280
http://www.awg.org

U.S. Department of Energy
(DOE)
Forrestal Building
100 Independence Avenue SW
Washington, D.C. 20585
http://www.doe.gov

International Association of
Drilling Contractors (IADC)
Houston Headquarters
P.O. Box 4287
Houston, Texas 77210-4287
http://www.iadc.org

National Petroleum Council
1625 K Street NW
Washington, D.C. 20006
http://www.npc.org

Pipeline Contractors
Association
1700 Pacific Avenue,
Suite 4100
Dallas, Texas 75201-4624

Society of Petroleum
Engineers (SPE)
P.O. Box 833836
222 Palisades Creek Drive
Richardson, Texas
75803-3836
http://www.spe.org

GET ACQUAINTED

David W. Lawrence,
Oil Rig Worker

CAREER PATH

CHILDHOOD ASPIRATION: To be a paleontologist.

FIRST JOB: Sales assistant in an auto parts store in Australia.

CURRENT JOB: Remote operated vehicle (ROV) pilot.

BE CAREFUL WHAT YOU WISH FOR

David Lawrence grew up in Australia and was introduced to the world of electronics when he was offered an apprenticeship with the phone company. He stayed with the company for seven years but decided he wanted to take some time off to see the world. His world travels took him to Hong Kong, where he played rugby, then on to Singapore, where he took a job painting for a guy who worked for a remote operated vehicle (ROV) company. The company made underwater robots used in oil rig drilling. With his background in electronics, it didn't take Lawrence long to figure out how they work—and within a week he was on a rig in Borneo.

ROVs were still new then—there were only 50 to 100 operators in the entire world. Now there are about 1,000. As a result, Lawrence often gets his pick of exotic places to work. So far, he's spent time on a rig in the North Sea off the shore of England, in Norway, the Middle East, the Indian Ocean, the Philippines, Japan, Korea, and the Gulf of Mexico. When he left Australia to see the world, Lawrence didn't expect to see quite so much of it!

A MAN WITH A PLAN

It takes more than an hour just to get a ROV to the proper depth and start to work, and it takes another hour just to get it back up to the surface again. That's why Lawrence has to know exactly what he's doing and how he's going to do it before he starts a job. All the necessary tools must be attached, its systems checked, and the task procedures practiced before the robot even touches the surface of the water.

THEY SAID IT COULDN'T BE DONE

Norway, near the Arctic Circle, was the site of one of the most exciting projects Lawrence has worked on so far. He was working on a huge concrete structure (three times the height of the Eiffel Tower, which is 300 meters or 984.25 feet!), and his job was to use the ROV to remove some panels on the ocean floor so the rig could be anchored. The engineers suggested some solutions. Helicopters flew back and forth bringing equipment and suggestions from the onshore experts. But no matter how hard the ROV pulled, the panels stayed firmly in place.

So Lawrence and his crew put their heads together and rigged a special tool for the ROV to use for twisting a bolt that held the panels in place. And, lo and behold, it worked. It felt pretty good to outsmart the experts for a change.

TREASURE HUNT

"ROV work isn't just on oil rigs," Lawrence says. Some of his friends work for companies that search for buried treasure and salvage sunken ships. One of the tasks they had was to find the HMS *Edinburgh,* an English warship sunk by a German U-boat during World War II. It had 60 tons of gold onboard to pay Russia for war materials. They flew in the ROV, found the ship, and helped to salvage the gold.

Paramedic

SHORTCUTS

GO take a class in first aid from the Red Cross.

READ *Paramedic: On the Front Lines of Medicine* by Peter Canning (New York: Ivy Books, 1998).

TRY visiting your local medical emergency response facility.

SKILL SET

✔ SCIENCE

✔ SPORTS

✔ ADVENTURE

WHAT IS A PARAMEDIC?

Accidents happen. And when they do, paramedics are often the professionals who are first on the scene. Paramedics or emergency medical technicians (EMTs) are the next best thing to having a doctor around when you're hurt. They can give drugs, interpret electrocardiograms, use defibrillators to restart hearts, perform minor medical procedures, deliver babies, and perform cardiopulmonary resuscitation (CPR). When someone is seriously injured or ill, time can make the difference between life and death. In many cases, quick response from paramedics literally saves lives.

A paramedic's job is to stabilize injured and ill patients and provide the urgent care they need until they can be safely transported to a hospital. In rural areas where the nearest hospital may be miles away, a paramedic may actually treat patients with a doctor giving instructions from another location until the patients can make a longer trip.

Paramedics have to be in good physical shape to do their jobs. On any given day, they may have to carry heavy packs of supplies, lift patients, and bend, kneel, and stand for long periods of time. They work in all kinds of weather. In fact, it's usually when the weather gets bad that accidents increase and paramedics are called in to help. Paramedics don't get "snow days." Their communities need them too much.

Many paramedics may work as part of an emergency response team. In ambulances fitted with sophisticated medical equipment and supplies, they rush to answer calls for help. Others are assigned to work with fire departments. Some are employed by hospitals and respond to emergency situations in "flight for life" helicopters.

Paramedics receive extensive first aid and medical training. They learn to recognize and respond to a wide variety of life-threatening situations. They must pass a series of written tests as well as a practical performance tests. There are three different levels of expertise for paramedics. The basic level requires 110 to 120 hours of classroom work, plus additional time spent working alongside doctors and nurses in the emergency room of a hospital. The intermediate level requires another 55 hours or more. A person is recognized as a full-fledged paramedic when he or she has received 2,000 hours of training.

Of course, in reality, the training never really stops. The field of medicine changes so rapidly that paramedics must work hard to stay up on the latest trends. To keep current, many paramedics devote 10 hours or more each month to training and staying abreast of new treatments, procedures, and drugs.

Training isn't the toughest part of the job. Most paramedics find that dealing with people in traumatic situations can get pretty stressful. This is not a job for those who faint at the sight of blood. Paramedics learn to approach even the most horrifying scenes calmly and competently. Compassion is essential, but paramedics can't let their emotions cloud their judgment. People count on them to know what they are doing and to do it as quickly and efficiently as possible.

Of course, all the hard work is worth it when a paramedic is able to save a life. Bringing a baby into the world, for instance, is one of the most rewarding parts of the job. Helping a small child in a car accident, saving a mother, listening as an asthmatic draws a deep breath after an attack—these are all things that make this career a very rewarding one.

TRY IT OUT

TAG ALONG
Since many paramedics operate out of fire stations, try visiting your local fire station. If you are old enough (most require you to be at least 13) and have your parents' permission, some fire stations will allow you to ride along on a few calls.

Other ways to get acquainted with the "tools" of this trade is to ask for a tour of an ambulance. There's a lot more to it than flashing red lights and a siren. Notice the different kinds of equipment they stock, and think about how it is arranged to fit a lot of supplies into a small space.

RED CROSS VOLUNTEER
Many Red Cross facilities have volunteer slots that kids can fill. You may have to take a first aid class, a CPR class, or a lifeguard class first. But any of these types of classes are great ways to learn how to help in emergency situation—and you never know when that knowledge will come in handy.

The Red Cross is on the scene of disasters around the world and has an almost endless need for committed volunteers. Get the training and find out how you can help.

To find your local Red Cross organization, check the business section of the phone book or go on-line to http://www.redcross.org.

GET PHYSICAL

Get in top physical shape. You must be able to do sit-ups and pull-ups, run up and down stairs quickly without getting tired, and generally be in peak condition. Take the tough physical education classes and get involved in sports to keep yourself ready.

TEST YOURSELF

Take the daily test put out by the National Center for Emergency Medicine Informatics at http://www.ncemi.org. It's a site used by real paramedics so it can get pretty technical, but you're sure to learn something if you snoop around a bit.

See if you can find out what to do in the following situations:

- You get a bloody nose.
- A friend gets stung by a bee.
- Your cousin sprains her ankle running the bases in a softball game.
- Your little brother mistakenly swallows some dish detergent.
- Your mom starts feeling faint while working in the yard on a hot day.

FIRST AID CROSSWORDS

Challenge yourself to find answers that lead to solutions in a series of fun first aid crossword puzzles. You'll find them on-line at http://homepage.virgin.net/stewart.watkiss/st_john/firstaid/is.fun/xwork/index.html.

One good place to hunt for answers is the Basic Home First Aid for Kids website at http://www.geocities.com/Athens/Academy/3483/kidsfirstaid.html.

CHECK IT OUT

Association of Emergency Physicians
127 Branchaw Boulevard
New Lenox, Illinois 60451
http://www.aep.org

Emergency Medicine Residents' Association
1125 Executive Circle
Irving, Texas 75038-2522
http://www.emra.org

National Association of Emergency Medical Technicians
408 Monroe
Clinton, Mississippi 39056

National Association of EMS Physicians
230 McKee Place, Suite 500
Pittsburgh, Pennsylvania 15213
http://www.pitt.edu/HOME/GHNet/naemsp/naemsp.html

National Emergency Medicine Association
306 West Joppa Road
Baltimore, Maryland 21204-4048
http://www.nemahealth.org

National Registry of Emergency Medical Technicians
P.O. Box 29233
Columbus, Ohio 43229

Safety Watch, Inc.
3140B Tilghman Street, PMB 256
Allentown, Pennsylvania 18104
http://www.safetywatchinc.con

Society for Academic Emergency Medicine
901 North Washington Avenue
Lansing, Michigan 48906-5137
http://www.saem.org

Society of Emergency Medicine Physician Assistants
950 North Washington Street
Alexandria, Virginia 22314-1552
http://www.sempa.org

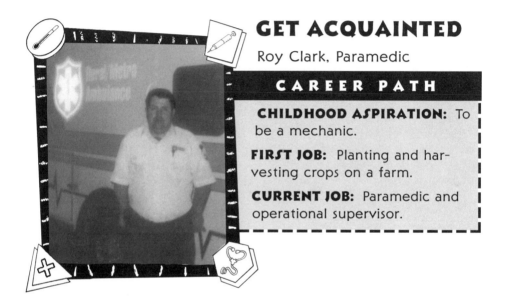

GET ACQUAINTED

Roy Clark, Paramedic

CAREER PATH

CHILDHOOD ASPIRATION: To be a mechanic.

FIRST JOB: Planting and harvesting crops on a farm.

CURRENT JOB: Paramedic and operational supervisor.

WHERE THERE'S A NEED

Roy Clark began his 20-year career as an emergency medical technician because he lived in a small town that needed an EMT. It was as simple as that. He wanted to make a difference in his community, and this job seemed like a good way to do it.

All the tests he had to take to become a paramedic stressed him out a bit. There were several levels, and he really wanted to pass. There were written tests and practical tests, requiring him to know such things as how and when to splint a patient, what medicines to administer, and how to assess a patient's problem. What a relief it was when he completed all those tests!

A CHILD IS BORN

Over the years, Clark has delivered many babies, including premature twins. While each delivery is special in its own way, he says that delivering his own son was incredible. Clark and his wife had planned for Clark to deliver their child so it wasn't quite as nerve-racking as it would have been if it had been an emergency. It was an incredible experience to bring his own child into the world. It's a memory he will always treasure.

TEARS AND CHEERS

Another time he was on a crew that transported a 105-year-old patient home after hip surgery. The smile on that patient's face as he got up and walked made Clark's day. It was great to see someone that age get a new lease on life.

Clark also remembers taking a 70-year-old cancer patient home. The woman knew she wouldn't live very much longer and told him she had always regretted not having grandchildren. Clark was so touched by this he went home and told his wife, who teaches Sunday school at their church. The kids in the Sunday school class wrote to the cancer patient, becoming her "grandchildren" for a while. Clark says that when he visited the patient a few days later, she had tears in her eyes.

HOOKED ON HELPING

The most exciting part of Clark's job is saving lives. He loves working with a team of emergency personnel to save someone who's been in an auto accident. It's great when this happens. Of course, the reverse is also true. When they do all they can to help but aren't able to save someone, the loss can be really tough to handle.

But just knowing he was there and did his best to give someone a chance helps Clark get through those sad endings. Thankfully, there are more happy endings than sad. And that is what makes this job so worthwhile for Clark and thousands of paramedics like him.

Ranch Hand

WHAT IS A RANCH HAND?

Better known as cowboys, ranch hands work on ranches raising animals, which will later be sold for food or breeding purposes. Things have changed quite a bit since the days of the Old West. Sure, there are plenty of fancy hats and horses to go around, but advances in technology have brought some interesting changes to the work.

For one thing, today's cowboy uses computers. Surprised? They use computers to keep track of the animals, maintaining such things as health records and feeding patterns. Computers even help ranch hands decide which pasture to use and which animals are to be sold and which are to breed. Of course, computers also help keep in order all the paperwork that comes with running a ranch. It's no longer enough to know how to lasso a cow, ranch hands have to master those computer skills, too.

Automobiles have also changed work on the ranch. Now a cowboy is just as likely to round up the cattle in a pickup truck as he or she is on horseback. With four-wheel drive trucks or all-terrain vehicles (ATVs), ranch hands can cover most of the same ground they could cover on horseback. Plus, there is plenty of room in the truck to carry bales of feed, tack, and other supplies, and it can also haul a stock trailer from one place to another.

Ranch Hand

Ranch hands need to know a lot about the animals they tend. Whether cows, sheep, emus, or buffalo, it's necessary to understand as much as possible about them. On any given day, a ranch hand may need to prepare feed mixes, repair equipment, manage the land, harvest grain and hay, or move a herd of animals from one pasture to another. It takes awhile to get the hang of everything, but a good ranch hand can generally be trusted to do it all.

Some ranches specialize in raising unusual animals, such as ostrich or emu, buffalo or elk. There are even salmon ranches and underwater ocean ranches raising crab, shrimp, and other types of fish. Variety is the name of the ranching game these days.

Ranch work involves a lot of hard physical tasks. Much of the work is done outdoors in all kinds of weather. Sometimes ranch hands actually live on the ranch itself in bunkhouses.

TRY IT OUT

CRITTER SITTER

One of the best ways to learn about what a ranch hand does is to take care of an animal or two. If you live on a farm or ranch already, this assignment will be a breeze. But what if you live in an apartment in the middle of a city or in a nice, quiet neighborhood that doesn't look kindly on ostriches in the backyard? You may have to scale back just a tad. Instead of a horse, try taking care of a dog or cat. Instead of an emu, try a hamster or parakeet. The idea here is to get used to the responsibility of caring for another creature. No matter what kind of animal you raise, you'll need to prepare a proper diet, feed at regular intervals, and clean up the inevitable messes. And, of course, you'll need permission from your parents first.

HOME, HOME ON THE WEB

Lasso a computer and see what kinds of information you can round up about ranchers and ranching. Here are a few website "pastures" to graze in:

- http://www.farmtimes.com
- http://www.usda.gov
- http://www.nacer.com
- http://www.modernsolutions.com/emu/ranch.html
- http://www.perc.org/hunting.htm
- http://www.ranchwest.com/problems.html

CHECK IT OUT

American Emu Association
P.O. Box 740814
Dallas, Texas 75374-0814
http://www.aea-emu.org

Bureau of Land Management
United States Department of the Interior
Office of Public Affairs

1849 C Street, Room 406-LS
Washington, D.C. 20240
http://www.blm.gov

United States Department of Agriculture
Jamie L. Whitten Building, 302-A
14th and Independence Avenue SW
Washington, D.C. 20250
http://www.ars.usda.gov

United States Forest Service
P.O. Box 96090
Washington, D.C. 20090-6090
http://www.fs.fed.us

GET ACQUAINTED

Coby Croft, Ranch Hand

CAREER PATH

CHILDHOOD ASPIRATION: To be an astronaut.

FIRST JOB: Mowing lawns.

CURRENT JOB: Ranch hand.

BORN TO RANCH

Coby Croft's family settled on a cattle ranch in Wyoming more than 100 years ago. As a young boy, he was expected to help out, doing chores that required progressively more responsibility from him. Over time, he's grown to love that land. Even though he occasionally takes a break from it to try new things, he knows he will always go back to the ranch.

One thing you can't get away from on a ranch is the sense of community. Croft says everyone pulls together. Everyone is expected to pull their own weight, but if someone gets hurt, lost, or stuck in a blizzard, the Crofts know they can depend on their neighbors to lend a hand. According to Coby, it's almost impossible to get into trouble without someone offering to help.

For instance, "The elderly man on the corner in town always seems to have his walk shoveled when it snows. He never does it himself. It just gets done." That's because people help one another in this small ranching town.

BEHIND THE WHEEL
Croft has always seemed to like trucks better than horses. Doing chores on the ranch, he was often behind the wheel of a pickup truck by the time he was 10 years old. Of course, he didn't drive anywhere except on the ranch, but he managed to put in lots of miles feeding and watering the animals and herding them around to different pastures.

RESPECT FOR THE LAND
Ranch hands tend to love working and playing outdoors, and Coby is no different. When chores are done, there's always a little time for some hunting and fishing.

A love for animals and nature is in his blood, and he takes every chance he gets to get out into the woods. "One time I was out fishing along the creek. I came upon a large moose cow with her calf. Of course, I turned and began to walk away," he says while assuring us that you "always walk, don't run" from dangerous animals. "She followed me for a good long ways before she turned back to where she'd left her calf."

He's encountered bears, too, while fishing: "In that case, you just lay your fish down and ease back down the road," Croft says.

A DIFFERENT KIND OF TEAMWORK

There isn't a typical day for a ranch hand. Each day is different. One day you might help a mother cow give birth to her calf. Another day you could be out moving cows from one range to another, vaccinating animals, or fixing broken equipment. According to Croft, "A rancher is always fixing something. You almost have to be a certified auto mechanic to make it. But, anybody can do this. Out here it doesn't matter whether you're a man or a woman, as long as you can do the job."

Teamwork is important too. A typical "team" might include a ranch hand, a horse, and a dog. Each plays a part in getting the job done and none of them could get it done without the others. That's teamwork! The ranch hand is the boss and is responsible for making sure his or her "teammates" are well cared for.

CRACK OF DAWN

The hours are sometimes a problem for Croft. As for most ranch hands, starting time is the crack of dawn and quitting time comes when the sun goes down. Dragging himself out a bed on a cold morning is sometimes, well, a "drag" for Croft. But the ranch won't wait. There are always animals to feed and chores to be done. Coby often works six or seven days a week, with no overtime pay, long hours in the summer, and short, boring hours in the winter.

Sometimes there just aren't enough hours in the day to get everything done. Twelve- and 14-hour days aren't unusual. "You spend the daylight hours with the animals, then after dinner, you sit at the computer looking at breeding schedules, shipping information, and health charts."

However, he feels it's all worth it. "Tending cows—slow elk, or hamburger-on-the-hoof, as we like to call them—just gives me a good excuse to get outdoors and marvel at the wonders of nature. Yes, you're bone tired at the end of the day, but you've had a great time."

Scuba Diver

WHAT IS A SCUBA DIVER?

Scuba divers work in underwater "offices." They use scuba (which stands for "self-contained underwater breathing apparatus") gear and other sophisticated equipment to explore the depths of the sea in a variety of scientific, commercial, and rescue endeavors.

Commercial divers work to support different kinds of projects such as construction, welding, engineering, and science. When you consider that everything they do is underwater, their feats are all the more amazing. Some divers work with scientists to explore the depths of various bodies of water or to gather research data on forms of sea life. Others work to salvage or recover sunken treasure or ships lost at sea. Still others work to build underwater pipelines or tunnels. Another diving specialty involves search-and-rescue missions, which generally occur when something has gone wrong above the water—a shipwreck or a plane crash, for example. In these instances, divers are racing against time to save lives, and their actions are often heroic. More underwater adventures come when scuba divers go down to inspect and videotape the undersides of large ships, build sea walls and docks, harvest seafood on a fish farm, and clean up contaminated waters.

Diving can be a dangerous job. There's no room for mistakes. While certain kinds of problems would be no big deal on dry land, they can turn fatal when you are working 150 feet below sea level. That's why planning plays such an important part in diver safety. A diver needs to think through the project, determine what tools are needed and how much air is required, and decide how long he or she can stay at a certain depth before coming up for air.

The most serious threat is pressure. As a diver descends into the ocean, the pressure increases. As the diver comes back up to sea level, air captured in the blood stream at the greater pressure expands and can cause a bad case of the "bends," an extremely painful and dangerous condition. Other threats come from strong currents and rough seas, cold temperatures, and low or no visibility. Feelings of isolation can also create mental stress. Curious fish—and sometimes even sharks—interfere with a diver working underwater.

Because of these hazards, divers are trained in cardiopulmonary resuscitation (CPR), first aid, proper diving techniques, the physics and physiology of diving, and the effects of pressure on the body. To become a commercial diver, you can train at a vocational-technical school, a certified dive

school, or in the U.S. Navy. You will need a high school diploma or its equivalent and expertise in your field of work, whether that's construction, engineering, science, or photography. You must also be at least 18 years old and have a doctor's certification that you are healthy enough to dive.

Most divers start out as tenders. These people do all the "topside" stuff out of the water such as maintaining communication with the diver, watching the diver's depth and the amount of air consumed, sending tools down, and retrieving items sent up by the diver. Tenders also run compressors and various pieces of equipment for the diver.

No doubt about it, scuba diving is a challenging and exciting career choice—just the thing for adventure lovers who are ready to get their feet wet.

TRY IT OUT

LIFE UNDER THE SEA
Imagine that you are going on an expedition to live at the bottom of the ocean (300 feet down) for three months. Make a list of everything you'll need (and want) to take with you. Don't forget your toothbrush!

To fuel your imagination, read the classic book *20,000 Leagues Under the Sea* by Jules Verne (New York: New American Library, 1993) or rent the movie version at your local video store.

SWIM WITH THE SHARKS
Are sharks evil, mean, bad, and nasty? Or are they just misunderstood? Peter Benchley wrote *Jaws,* a book about sharks which later became a movie. Since then, he has been doing research on the great white creatures of the deep. *National Geographic* magazine's April 2000 issue takes a closer look at these integral members of the ocean's food chain. Find out about their habits, their normal prey, and their susceptibility to extinction. What would you do if you were scuba diving and a shark swam by?

DIVE INTO THE WEB

The Internet provides some fun resources for underwater exploration. You don't even have to get wet at websites such as these:

- http://www.scubayellowpages.com/misclinks/misc.htm where you'll find links to all kinds of cool diving information
- http://naocd.org/schools.htm for the lowdown on commercial diving
- http://www.dolphinlog.org for a virtual swim with the dolphins
- http://nationalgeographic.com and click on "Kids" for a dive in beautiful Monterey Bay in California

CHECK IT OUT

Association of Diving Contractors International
3910 FM 1960 West, Suite 230
Houston, Texas 77068
http://www.adc-usa.org

Center for Marine Conservation
1725 DeSales Street NW, Suite 600
Washington, D.C. 20036
http://www.cmc-ocean.org

Commercial Dive Safety Organization
3285 126th Avenue NE
Bellevue, Washington 98005
http://www.safedive.org

Commercial Divers International, Inc.
5093 White Pine Circle
St. Petersburg, Florida 33703
http://www.comdivers.com

The Cousteau Society
870 Greenbrier Circle, Suite 402
Chesapeake, Virginia 23320
http://cousteausociety.org

Dive Rescue International
201 North Link Lane
Fort Collins, Colorado 80524-2712
http://www.diverescueintl.com

Handicapped Scuba Association International
1104 El Prado
San Clemente, California 92572-4637
http://www.hsascuba.com

International Association of Dive Rescue Specialists
P.O. Box 479
Windsor, Colorado 80550
http://www.iadrs.org

International Association of Nitrox and Technical Divers, Inc.
9628 NE Second Avenue, Suite D
Miami Shores, Florida 33138-2767
http://www.iantd.com

National Association of Commercial Divers
P.O. Box 915
Charlottesville, Virginia 22902-0915
http://naocd.org

National Association of Underwater Instructors (NAUI)
9942 Currie David Drive, Suite H
Tampa, Florida 33619-2667
http://www.naui.org

Professional Association of Diving Instructors (PADI) Worldwide
    Headquarters
1251 East Dyer Road, #100
Santa Ana, California 92705
http://www.padi.com

Technical Diving International (TDI)
Nine Coastal Plaza, Suite 300
Bath, Maine 04530
http://www.techdiver.com

YMCA National Scuba Program
5825-2A Live Oak Parkway
Norcross, Georgia 30093
http://www.ymcascuba.org

GET ACQUAINTED

Dan Petit, Scuba Diver

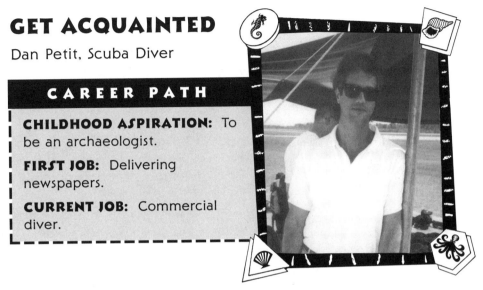

CAREER PATH

CHILDHOOD ASPIRATION: To be an archaeologist.

FIRST JOB: Delivering newspapers.

CURRENT JOB: Commercial diver.

ADVENTURE-BOUND

While still in high school, Dan Petit became certified as a scuba diver just for fun. When it came time to choose a career, he knew that he didn't want to go to college and he did want lots of adventure. After reading some ads for commercial divers in a skindivers' magazine, he knew he was onto something. The idea of getting paid to go underwater sounded terrific. He got himself in shape, saved his money, and went to dive school to get certified as a commercial diver. He worked for 20 years as a successful commercial diver before recently retiring.

"Diving is hard on your body, so even before you reach 40, you're ready to retire." He still works in the diving industry, however. Petit spends his days working for a company that sends divers and underwater robots down to build oil rig structures and pipelines.

MOVE OVER, ROVER

Sometimes sea creatures get in the way of a diver's work. "I'd be down there trying to do some welding, and sharks and eels would keep bumping me. Once, when I was diving at the mouth of the Mississippi, a small shark kept swimming in between my hands. I never knew when he was coming. Between what he was doing and the eels that kept bumping into me, I got very little done that day."

Another time, when he was diving in the Gulf of Mexico, Petit remembers, "I was suited up and ready to go down to relieve another diver. I was watching the guy that was already down there as he worked. The camera showed several large sharks that kept hitting him." Then it was Petit's turn to go down. He took it easy, being just a little "respectful" of them. As Petit recalls, it was one dive that he couldn't finish quickly enough!

MUD BUGS

Commercial divers do a lot of their work in mud. They sink into the muck with every step. Of course, all the mud churns up as they work, making it difficult or impossible to see what they're doing. Drop a tool, and it's gone for good. Petit says that when working in the mud, you have to operate by feel. It's like trying to put together a puzzle with your eyes closed!

Welder

WHAT IS A WELDER?

Under certain conditions, heat and pressure combine to fuse metal together in an extremely strong and long-lasting bond. Welders use this technique in many ways. Whether it's constructing a tall skyscraper, building a bridge for a train track, piecing together a ship's hull, or putting together a hydro-dam filtration system, welders use special equipment and technical skill to connect metals.

There are different kinds of welding techniques for different kinds of jobs. The most common techniques are gas metal arc welding (MIG), gas tungsten arc welding (TIG), flux cored welding, shielded metal arc welding (stick electrode), and resistance welding. Welding can also be done using an explosion method or laser beams.

Welders work on all sorts of interesting projects involving anything from spacecraft, ships, and automobiles to pipelines, nuclear power plants, and skyscrapers. For some custom jobs, they weld manually using a blowtorch and other tools. In some manufacturing situations, repetitive welding tasks may be automated by using robots.

There are more than 475,000 people working as welders in the United States. Most of them work in just six states that have heavy automobile manufacturing or oil and gas exploration operations. You don't have to go to college to become a welder. But you do need to take welding classes in high

school or at a vocational-technical school and get plenty of on-the-job training. Some people work as welders in the military and get good training there.

Good welders take the time to do the job right. Welding takes concentration and attention to detail. Welders must be able to read plans and drawings and make math calculations to work with precise measurements.

By no means is welding considered a "desk job." Depending on the situation, a welder might be working in any number of physically challenging positions—sitting, standing, or lying down in a cramped space. Some welders who are certified as divers even work underwater.

Safety is a big issue for this job. Welders wear protective clothing, safety shoes, goggles, hoods with protective lenses, and face shields, and they must have adequate ventilation. Sparks fly when welders work. So every precaution must be taken to prevent getting burned.

Robots and computers meet more and more welding needs as new strides are made in technology. Undersea welding is a growing area for welders, as is working in the aerospace industry. Because our society is so dependent on metals, we can be sure that we won't run out of opportunities for welders—both mechanical and human.

TRY IT OUT

STUCK ON YOU

Due to safety considerations, you can't just run out and give welding a try. But you can get the general idea of the welding process by doing a little experiment with different kinds of glue.

Enlist the help of an adult to help you gather several different kinds of objects that you can glue together. Get scraps of paper, fabric, cardboard, metal, and plastic. Now get some regular school glue, some rubber cement, and some heavy-duty, permanent adhesive glue. Use the different kinds of glue to "fuse" different kinds of materials together. Try fusing the materials at different angles. Notice which glues work best with which materials.

Welding works a lot like glue—different kinds of materials and techniques work better in different kinds of situation.

TAKE THE "FIND A WELD" CHALLENGE

How many things can you find that are made out of metal in your home? At your school? Around town? Make a list and then examine each object carefully to find places where metals have been welded together. Keep track of how many welds you can find. Bet you find at least a dozen!

ARC INTO CYBERSPACE

It's amazing what you can find on the Internet. There's even some good stuff about welding to be found at sites like those described below.

For a list of lots of welding associations, institutes, and societies, go to http://www.ewi.org/resources/society.html.

Read about explosive bonding at http://www.highenergymetals.com.

Check out the kids' page on the United Association of Journeymen and Apprentices of the Plumbing and Pipefitting Industry of the United States and Canada at http://www.ua.org/ua_kids.htm.

CHECK IT OUT

American Institute of Steel
    Construction
One East Wacker Drive,
    Suite 3100
Chicago, Illinois 60601-2001
http://www.aisc.org

American Welding Society
550 North West LeJeune Road
Miami, Florida 33126-5699
http://www.amweld.org

International Association of
    Machinists and Aerospace
    Workers
9000 Machinists Place
Upper Marlboro, Maryland
    20772-2687
http://www.iamaw.org

International Brotherhood of
    Boilermakers, Iron Ship
    Builders, Blacksmiths,
    Forgers and Helpers, AFL-CIO
753 State Avenue
Kansas City, Kansas 66101
http://www.boilermakers.org

Sheet Metal Workers'
    International Association
601 North Fairfax Street,
    Suite 240
Alexandria, Virginia 22314
http://www.smwia.org

United Association of
    Journeymen and Apprentices
    of the Plumbing and
    Pipefitting Industry of the
    United States and Canada
901 Massachusetts Avenue NW
Washington, D.C. 20001
http://www.ua.org

United Automobile, Aerospace
    & Agricultural Implement
    Workers of America
P.O. Box 6876
St. Louis Missouri 63108
http://www.uawndm.com

GET ACQUAINTED

Kandy Knott, Welder

CAREER PATH

CHILDHOOD ASPIRATION: To be an accountant.

FIRST JOB: Baby-sitting.

CURRENT JOB: Sheet metal welder.

ALL IN THE FAMILY

Growing up, Kandy Knott loved math. She thought for a while about becoming an accountant. But since Knott's grandfather owned a welding shop and her mother worked as a welder, it was only natural that as Knott got older she started helping out at the shop from time to time. She would repair the aluminum fuel tanks and do other odd jobs.

One thing led to another, and after a while she went to work for another company as a sheet metal welder. Her training has been on the job, but all that early experience sure has come in handy.

WOMEN CAN WELD, TOO!

Welding has traditionally been a "man's job." So even now Knott is the only woman working at her shop. But it hasn't been a problem. She feels that she works a little harder to get things done just right and seems to have a steadier hand.

Does she get any ribbing? "Just the opposite. I feel great when I can say I'm a woman welder," she says. "I take pride in my work. It's nice to be able to finish the job, stand back, and say to myself 'I did that,' knowing it will last for a long time."

ADVENTURES IN WELDING

Knott's job is full of variety. From countertops to sinks to gates, she rarely knows from one day to the next what she'll be working on. And welding isn't the only thing she does. She also gets to interact with the customers and make suggestions about ways to fabricate a piece to make it last longer.

Sometimes, she isn't quite sure what she's working on. "I try to ask, but sometimes I just see the plans and have to make what's there. I worked on a 4-feet-by-4-feet-by-4-feet stainless steel box just recently. I had no clue where it was going or what it would do. I just knew it was going to be used in a dam somewhere. My welds were good, and I guess that's the important part for me."

HOT STUFF

The toughest part of Knott's job is the physical demands. Metal is heavy. She mainly works with aluminum, steel, or stainless steel plates that measure 4 feet by 10 feet. There's a lot of lifting involved, and for the most part she's on her own. Her job results in a lot of firm muscles!

The work also takes quite a bit of coordination. Sometimes Knott finds herself working with equipment in both hands and one foot on a foot pedal. It's almost like being a drummer in a band!

The protective gear she has to wear means both good news and bad news. The good news is that it keeps her safe, and she wouldn't dare work without it. The bad news is that it gets hot when you're wrapped from head to toe in protective clothing. By the end of the day, Knott is ready to hit the shower!

A FAMILY TRADITION

One of the best things about Knott's work is that she is able to carry on the tradition of excellence started by her grandfather so many years ago and continued by her mother. And even though her son is too small for welding just yet, Knott hopes that he might someday carry on the tradition for another generation.

MAKE AN ADVENTURE-FILLED DETOUR!

Who says work has to be boring? Match your skills and interests with an adventurous career idea and you could be in for a thrill a minute. OK, maybe not every single minute will be incredibly exciting. But find a career that challenges you to be all that you can possibly be—and a little more—and you will find something worth keeping.

MORE EXCITING CAREER CHOICES

THE SCIENCE OF ADVENTURE

Adventure lovers everywhere make sure to consider a career in science. It's hard to find another field that offers so many opportunities for discovery and challenge. Here are just a few ideas to get you thinking.

aerospace engineer	environmentalist
anthropologist	epidemiologist
archaeologist	geographer
astronomer	geologist
biologist	marine biologist
botanist	nuclear physicist
ecologist	petroleum engineer

ANIMAL ADVENTURES

If you've ever tried to train a puppy, you know that having anything to do with animals can be a real adventure. Following are some ways to make animals a part of your adventurous career.

animal ecologist	horse trainer
animal scientist	lion tamer
circus performer	veterinarian
exotic animal trainer	zookeeper
farmer	

AROUND-THE-WORLD ADVENTURES

Here are some ways to work your way around the world.

air traffic controller	race car driver
cruise director	sailor
deep sea fisherman	sea captain
diplomat	tour guide
flight attendant	travel agent
helicopter pilot	truck driver
merchant marine	

HANDS-ON ADVENTURES

There's nothing quite as satisfying as working with your own two hands. Here are some ideas to combine special skills with making a living.

bricklayer
cabinetmaker
cable installer
concrete mason
electrician
flooring installer

heating and air-conditioning
   installer
ironworker
pipefitter
plasterer
stonemason
window washer

OUT-OF-THIS-WORLD ADVENTURE

You're sure to find plenty of adventure to go around in any of these space-related career ideas.

aerospace engineer
mission control specialist
satellite designer
satellite operator

spacecraft simulation engineer
space launch specialist
spacesuit designer

HELPFUL ADVENTURES

Doing good can be a good way to earn your keep. These careers feature opportunities to help others in one way or another.

bomb squad officer
fire marshal
personal trainer
police officer
politician
psychiatrist
psychologist
sports physician
storm chaser

INFORMATION IS POWER

Mind-boggling, isn't it? There are so many great choices, so many jobs you've never heard of before. How will you ever narrow it down to the perfect spot for you?

First, pinpoint the ideas that sound the most interesting to you. Then, find out all you can about them. As you may have noticed, a similar pattern of information was used for each of the career entries featured in this book. Each entry included

- ☼ a general description or definition of the career
- ☼ some hands-on projects that give readers a chance to actually experience a job
- ☼ a list of organizations to contact for more information
- ☼ an interview with a professional

You can use information like this to help you determine the best career path to pursue. Since there isn't room in one book to profile all these math-related career choices, here's your chance to do it yourself. Conduct a full investigation into an adventure-filled career that interests you.

Please Note: If this book does not belong to you, use a separate sheet of paper to record your responses to the following questions.

CAREER TITLE _____

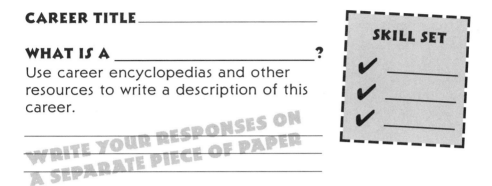

WHAT IS A _____?
Use career encyclopedias and other resources to write a description of this career.

SKILL SET

✔ _____

✔ _____

✔ _____

TRY IT OUT
Write project ideas here. Ask your parents and your teacher to come up with a plan.

CHECK IT OUT
List professional organizations where you can learn more about this profession.

GET ACQUAINTED
Interview a professional in the field and summarize your findings.

DON'T STOP NOW!

GO FOR IT!

It's been a fast-paced trip so far. Take a break, regroup, and look at all the progress you've made.

1st Stop: Self-Discovery
You discovered some personal interests and natural abilities that you can start building a career around.

2nd Stop: Exploration
You've explored an exciting array of adventure-filled career opportunities. You're now aware that your career can involve either a specialized area with many educational requirements or that it can involve a practical application of skills with a minimum of training and experience.

At this point, you've found a couple of (or few) careers that really intrigue you. Now it's time to put it all together and do all you can to make an informed, intelligent choice. It's time to move on.

3rd Stop: Experimentation

By the time you finish this section, you'll have reached one of three points in the career planning process.

1. **Green light!** You found it. No need to look any further. This is *the* career for you. (This may happen to a lucky few. Don't worry if it hasn't happened yet for you. This whole process is about exploring options, experimenting with ideas, and, eventually, making the best choice for you.)
2. **Yellow light!** Close, but not quite. You seem to be on the right path but you haven't nailed things down for sure. (This is where many people your age end up, and it's a good place to be. You've learned what it takes to really check things out. Hang in there. Your time will come.)
3. **Red light!** Whoa! No doubt about it, this career just isn't for you. (Congratulations! Aren't you glad you found out now and not after you'd spent four years in college preparing for this career? Your next stop: Make a U-turn and start this process over with another career.)

Here's a sneak peek at what you'll be doing in the next section.

☀ First, you'll pick a favorite career idea (or two or three).
☀ Second, you'll snoop around the library to find answers to the 10 things you've just got to know about your future career.
☀ Third, you'll pick up the phone and talk to someone whose career you admire to find out what it's really like.
☀ Fourth, you'll link up with a whole world of great information about your career idea on the Internet (it's easier than you think).
☀ Fifth, you'll go on the job to shadow a professional for a day.

Hang on to your hats and get ready to make tracks!

#1 NARROW DOWN YOUR CHOICES

You've been introduced to quite a few exciting career ideas. You may also have some ideas of your own to add. Which ones appeal to you the most?

Write your top three choices in the spaces below. (Sorry if this is starting to sound like a broken record, but . . . **if this book does not belong to you, write your responses on a separate sheet of paper.**)

1. _____
2. _____
3. _____

WRITE YOUR RESPONSES ON
A SEPARATE PIECE OF PAPER

#2 SNOOP AT THE LIBRARY

Take your list of favorite career ideas, a notebook, and a helpful adult with you to the library. When you get there, go to the reference section and ask the librarian to help you find books about careers. Most libraries will have at least one set of career encyclopedias. Some of the larger libraries may also have career information on CD-ROM.

Gather all the information you can and use it to answer the following questions in your notebook about each of the careers on your list. Make sure to ask for help if you get stuck.

TOP 10 THINGS YOU NEED TO KNOW ABOUT YOUR CAREER

1. What kinds of skills does this job require?
2. What kind of training is required? (Compare the options for a high school degree, trade school degree, two-year degree, four-year degree, and advanced degree.)
3. What types of classes do I need to take in high school in order to be accepted into a training program?
4. What are the names of three schools or colleges where I can get the training I need?
5. Are there any apprenticeship or internship opportunities available? If so, where? If not, could I create my own opportunity? How?
6. How much money can I expect to earn as a beginner? How much with more experience?
7. What kinds of places hire people to do this kind of work?
8. What is a typical work environment like? For example, would I work in a busy office, outdoors, or in a laboratory?
9. What are some books and magazines I could read to learn more about this career? Make a list and look for them at your library.
10. Where can I write for more information? Make a list of professional associations.

#3 CHAT ON THE PHONE

Talking to a seasoned professional—someone who experiences the job day in and day out—can be a great way to get the inside story on what a career is all about. Fortunately for you, the experts in any career field can be as close as the nearest telephone.

Sure it can be a bit scary calling up an adult whom you don't know. But, two things are in your favor:

1. They can't see you. The worst thing they can do is hang up on you, so just relax and enjoy the conversation.
2. They'll probably be happy to talk to you about their job. In fact, most people will be flattered that you've called. If you happen to contact someone who seems reluctant to talk, thank them for their time and try someone else.

Here are a few pointers to help make your telephone interview a success.

- ☼ Mind your manners and speak clearly.
- ☼ Be respectful of their time and position.
- ☼ Be prepared with good questions and take notes as you talk.

One more commonsense reminder: Be careful about giving out your address and DO NOT arrange to meet anyone you don't know without your parents' supervision.

TRACKING DOWN CAREER EXPERTS

You might be wondering by now how to find someone to interview. Have no fear! It's easy, if you're persistent. All you have to do is ask. Ask the right people and you'll have a great lead in no time.

A few of the people to ask and sources to turn to are

Your parents. They may know someone (or know someone who knows someone) who has just the kind of job you're looking for.

Your friends and neighbors. You might be surprised to find out how many interesting jobs these people have when you start asking them what they (or their parents) do for a living.

Librarians. Since you've already figured out what kinds of companies employ people in your field of interest, the next step is to ask for information about local employers. Although it's a bit cumbersome to use, a big volume called *Contacts Influential* can provide this kind of information.

Professional associations. Call or write to the professional associations you discovered in Activity #1 a few pages back and ask for recommendations.

Chambers of commerce. The local chamber of commerce probably has a directory of employers, their specialties, and their phone numbers. Call the chamber, explain what you are looking for, and give the person a chance to help the future workforce.

Newspaper and magazine articles. Find an article about the subject you are interested in. Chances are pretty good that it will mention the name of at least one expert in the field. The article probably won't include the person's phone number (that would be too easy), so you'll have to look for clues. Common clues include the name of the company that the expert works for, the town that he or she lives in, and if the person is an author, the name of his or her publisher. Make a few phone calls and track the person down (if long distance calls are involved, make sure to get your parents' permission first).

INQUIRING KIDS WANT TO KNOW

Before you make the call, make a list of questions to ask. You'll cover more ground if you focus on using the five w's (and the h) that you've probably heard about in your creative writing classes: Who? What? Where? When? How? and Why? For example,

1. Who do you work for?
2. What is a typical work day like for you?
3. Where can I get some on-the-job experience?
4. When did you become a _____?
   (profession)
5. How much can you earn in this profession? (But, remember it's not polite to ask someone how much *he* or *she* earns.)
6. Why did you choose this profession?

One last suggestion: Add a professional (and very classy) touch to the interview process by following up with a thank-you note to the person who took time out of a busy schedule to talk with you.

#4 SURF THE NET

With the Internet, the new information super-highway, charging full steam ahead, you literally have a world of information at your fingertips. The Internet has something for everyone, and it's getting easier to access all the time. An increasing number of libraries and schools are

offering access to the Internet on their computers. In addition, companies such as America Online and CompuServe have made it possible for anyone with a home computer to surf the World Wide Web.

A typical career search will land everything from the latest news on developments in the field and course notes from universities to museum exhibits, interactive games, educational activities, and more. You just can't beat the timeliness or the variety of information available on the Net.

One of the easiest ways to track down this information is to use an Internet search engine, such as Yahoo! Simply type in the topic you are looking for, and in a matter of seconds, you'll have a list of options from around the world. It's fun to browse—you never know what you'll come up with.

To narrow down your search a bit, look for specific websites, forums, or chatrooms that are related to your topic in the following publications:

Hahn, Harley. *Harley Hahn's Internet and Web Yellow Pages.* Berkeley, Calif.: Osborne McGraw Hill, 1999.
Turner, Marcia Layton, and Audrey Seybold. *Official World Wide Web Yellow Pages.* Indianapolis: Que, 1999.
Polly, Jean Armour. *The Internet Kids and Family Yellow Pages.* Berkeley, Calif.: Osborne McGraw Hill, 1999.

To go on-line at home you may want to compare two of the more popular on-line services: America Online and CompuServe. Please note that there is a monthly subscription fee for using these services. There can also be extra fees attached to specific forums and services, so *make sure you have your parents' OK before you sign up.* For information about America Online call 800-827-6364. For information about CompuServe call 800-848-8990. Both services frequently offer free start-up deals, so shop around.

There are also many other services, depending on where you live. Check your local phone book or ads in local computer magazines for other service options.

Before you link up, keep in mind that many of these sites are geared toward professionals who are already working in a particular field. Some of the sites can get pretty technical. Just use the experience as a chance to nose around the field, hang out with the people who are tops in the field, and think about whether or not you'd like to be involved in a profession like that.

Specific sites to look for are the following:

Professional associations. Find out about what's happening in the field, conferences, journals, and other helpful tidbits.

Schools that specialize in this area. Many include research tools, introductory courses, and all kinds of interesting information.

Government agencies. Quite a few are going high-tech with lots of helpful resources.

Websites hosted by experts in the field (this seems to be a popular hobby among many professionals). These websites are often as entertaining as they are informative.

If you're not sure where to go, just start clicking around. Sites often link to other sites. You may want to jot down notes about favorite sites. Sometimes you can even print out information that isn't copyright-protected; try the print option and see what happens.

Be prepared: Surfing the Internet can be an addicting habit! There is so much great information. It's a fun way to focus on your future.

#5 SHADOW A PROFESSIONAL

Linking up with someone who is gainfully employed in a profession that you want to explore is a great way to find out what a career is like. Following someone around while the person are at work is called "shadowing." Try it!

This process involves three steps.

1. Find someone to shadow. Some suggestions include
   - ☼ the person you interviewed (if you enjoyed talking with him or her and feel comfortable about asking the person to show you around the workplace)
   - ☼ friends and neighbors (you may even be shocked to discover that your parents have interesting jobs)
   - ☼ workers at the chamber of commerce may know of mentoring programs available in your area (it's a popular concept, so most larger areas should have something going on)
   - ☼ someone at your local School-to-Work office, the local Boy Scouts Explorer program director (this is available to girls too!), or your school guidance counselor
2. Make a date. Call and make an appointment. Find out when is the best time for arrival and departure. Make arrangements with a parent or other respected adult to go with you and get there on time.
3. Keep your ears and eyes open. This is one time when it is OK to be nosy. Ask

questions. Notice everything that is happening around you. Ask your host to let you try some of the tasks he or she is doing.

The basic idea of the shadowing experience is to put yourself in the other person's shoes and see how they fit. Imagine yourself having a job like this 10 or 15 years down the road. It's a great way to find out if you are suited for a particular line of work.

BE CAREFUL OUT THERE!

Two cautions must accompany this recommendation. First, remember the stranger danger rules of your childhood. NEVER meet with anyone you don't know without your parents' permission and ALWAYS meet in a supervised situation— at the office or with your parents.

Second, be careful not to overdo it. These people are busy earning a living, so respect their time by limiting your contact and coming prepared with valid questions and background information.

PLAN B

If shadowing opportunities are limited where you live, try one of these approaches for learning the ropes from a professional.

Pen pals. Find a mentor who is willing to share information, send interesting materials, or answer specific questions that come up during your search.

Cyber pals. Go on-line in a forum or chatroom related to the profession you're interested in. You'll be able to chat with professionals from all over the world.

If you want to get some more on-the-job experience, try one of these approaches.

Volunteer to do the dirty work. Volunteer to work for someone who has a job that interests you for a specified period of time. Do anything—filing, errands, emptying trash cans—that puts you in contact with professionals. Notice every tiny detail about the profession. Listen to the lingo they use in the profession. Watch how they perform their jobs on a day-to-day basis.

Be an apprentice. This centuries-old job training method is making a comeback. Find out if you can set up an official on-the-job training program to gain valuable experience. Ask professional associations about apprenticeship opportunities. Once again, a School-to-Work program can be a great asset. In many areas, they've established some very interesting career training opportunities.

Hire yourself for the job. Maybe you are simply too young to do much in the way of on-the-job training right now. That's OK. Start learning all you can now and you'll be ready to really wow them when the time is right. Make sure you do all the Try It Out activities included for the career(s) you are most interested in. Use those activities as a starting point for creating other projects that will give you a feel for what the job is like.

WHAT'S NEXT?

Have you carefully worked your way through all of the suggested activities? You haven't tried to sneak past anything, have you? This isn't a place for shortcuts. If you've done the activities, you're ready to decide where you stand with each career idea. So what is it? Green light? See page 158. Yellow light? See page 157. Red light? See page 156. Find the spot that best describes your response to what you've discovered about this career idea and plan your next move.

RED LIGHT

So you've decided this career is definitely not for you—hang in there! The process of elimination is an important one. You've learned some valuable career planning skills; use them to explore other ideas. In the meantime, use the following road map to chart a plan to get beyond this "spinning your wheels" point in the process.

Take a variety of classes at school to expose yourself to new ideas and expand the options. Make a list of courses you want to try.

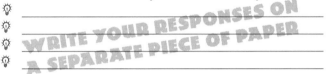

Get involved in clubs and other after-school activities (like 4-H or Boy Scout Explorers) to further develop your interests. Write down some that interest you.

Read all you can find about interesting people and their work. Make a list of people you'd like to learn more about.

WRITE YOUR RESPONSES ON A SEPARATE PIECE OF PAPER

Keep at it. Time is on your side. Finding the perfect work for you is worth a little effort. Once you've crossed this hurdle, move on to the next pages and continue mapping out a great future.

YELLOW LIGHT

Proceed with caution. While the idea continues to intrigue you, you may wonder if it's the best choice for you. Your concerns are legitimate (listen to that nagging little voice inside!).

Maybe it's the training requirements that intimidate you. Maybe you have concerns about finding a good job once you complete the training. Maybe you wonder if you have what it takes to do the job.

At this point, it's good to remember that there is often more than one way to get somewhere. Check out all the choices and choose the route that's best for you. Use the following road map to move on down the road in your career planning adventure.

Make two lists. On the first, list the things you like most about the career you are currently investigating. On the second, list the things that are most important to you in a future career. Look for similarities on both lists and focus on careers that emphasize these similar key points.

Current Career	Future Career
☼ _____	☼ _____
☼ _____	☼ _____

What are some career ideas that are similar to the one you have in mind? Find out all you can about them. Go back through the exploration process explained on pages 139 to 148 and repeat some of the exercises that were most valuable.

☼ _____
☼ _____
☼ _____
☼ _____

Visit your school counselor and ask him or her which career assessment tools are available through your school. Use these to find out more about your strengths and interests. List the date, time, and place for any assessment tests you plan to take.

What other adults do you know and respect to whom you can talk about your future? They may have ideas that you've never thought of.

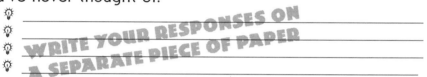

What kinds of part-time jobs, volunteer work, or after-school experiences can you look into that will give you a chance to build your skills and test your abilities? Think about how you can tap into these opportunities.

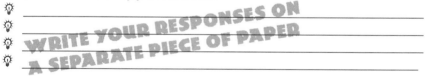

GREEN LIGHT

Yahoo! You are totally turned on to this career idea and ready to do whatever it takes to make it your life's work. Go for it!

Find out what kinds of classes you need to take now to pre-pare for this career. List them here.

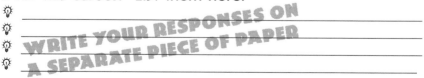

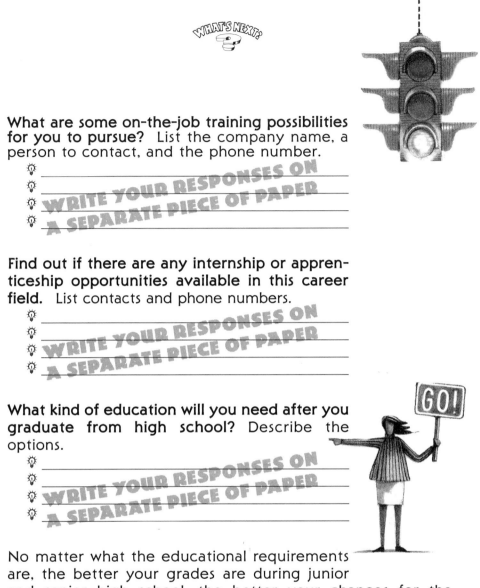

What are some on-the-job training possibilities for you to pursue? List the company name, a person to contact, and the phone number.

WRITE YOUR RESPONSES ON A SEPARATE PIECE OF PAPER

Find out if there are any internship or apprenticeship opportunities available in this career field. List contacts and phone numbers.

WRITE YOUR RESPONSES ON A SEPARATE PIECE OF PAPER

What kind of education will you need after you graduate from high school? Describe the options.

WRITE YOUR RESPONSES ON A SEPARATE PIECE OF PAPER

No matter what the educational requirements are, the better your grades are during junior and senior high school, the better your chances for the future.

Take a minute to think about some areas that need improvement in your schoolwork. Write your goals for giving it all you've got here.

WRITE YOUR RESPONSES ON A SEPARATE PIECE OF PAPER

Where can you get the training you'll need? Make a list of colleges, technical schools, or vocational programs. Include addresses so that you can write to request a catalog.

WRITE YOUR RESPONSES ON
A SEPARATE PIECE OF PAPER

HOORAY! YOU DID IT!

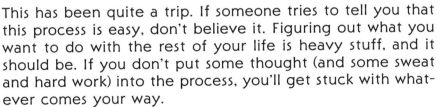

This has been quite a trip. If someone tries to tell you that this process is easy, don't believe it. Figuring out what you want to do with the rest of your life is heavy stuff, and it should be. If you don't put some thought (and some sweat and hard work) into the process, you'll get stuck with whatever comes your way.

You may not have things planned to a T. Actually, it's probably better if you don't. You'll change some of your ideas as you grow and experience new things. And, you may find an interesting detour or two along the way. That's OK.

The most important thing about beginning this process now is that you've started to dream. You've discovered that you have some unique talents and abilities to share. You've become aware of some of the ways you can use them to make a living—and, perhaps, make a difference in the world.

Whatever you do, don't lose sight of the hopes and dreams you've discovered. You've got your entire future ahead of you. Use it wisely.

SOME FUTURE DESTINATIONS

Wow! You've really made tracks during this whole process. Now that you've gotten this far, you'll want to keep moving forward to a great future. This section will point you toward some useful resources to help you make a conscientious career choice (that's just the opposite of falling into any old job on a fluke).

IT'S NOT JUST FOR NERDS

The school counselor's office is not just a place where teachers send troublemakers. One of its main purposes is to help students like you make the most of your educational opportunities. Most schools will have a number of useful resources, including career assessment tools (ask about the Self-Directed Search Career Explorer or the COPS Interest Inventory—these are especially useful assessments for people your age). There may also be a stash of books, videos, and other helpful materials.

Make sure no one's looking and sneak into your school counseling office to get some expert advice!

AWESOME INTERNET CAREER RESOURCES

Your parents will be green with envy when they see all the career planning resources you have at your fingertips. Get ready to hear them whine, "But they didn't have all this stuff when I was a kid." Make the most of these cyberspace opportunities.

- ☼ Future Scan includes in-depth profiles on a wide variety of career choices and expert advice from their "Guidance Gurus." Check it out at http://www.futurescan.com.
- ☼ For up-to-the-minute news on what's happening in the world of work, visit Career Magazine's website at http://www.careermag.com.
- ☼ Monster.com, one of the web's largest job search resources, hosts a site called Monster Campus at http://campus.monster.com. There's all kinds of career information, college stuff, and links to jobs, jobs, jobs!
- ☼ Find links to all kinds of career information at http://careerplanning.about.com. You'll have to use your best detective skills to find what you want, but there is a lot of good information to be found on this site.

- Even Uncle Sam wants to help you find a great career. Check out the Department of Labor's Occupational Outlook Handbook for in-depth information on approximately 250 occupations at http://www.bls. gov./ocohome.htm.
- Buffalo State University hosts an exceptionally good career exploration website. Find it at http://www.sny-buf.edu.~cdc/explore.html.
- Another fun site for the inside scoop on a wide variety of career options is found at http://www.jobprofiles. com.
- Pick a favorite career and find out specific kinds of information such as wages and trends at http://www.acinet. org/acinet/occ_seal.htm.

IT'S NOT JUST FOR BOYS

Boys and girls alike are encouraged to contact their local version of the Boy Scouts Explorer program. It offers exciting on-the-job training experiences in a variety of professional fields. Look in the white pages of your community phone book for the local Boy Scouts of America program.

MORE CAREER BOOKS ESPECIALLY FOR ADVENTURE FREAKS

If adventure is your thing, you don't have to settle for a humdrum job. There are a surprising number of ways to mix the thrill of adventure with your life's work. The following books provide more information about additional exciting career options.

Field, Shelly. *The Unofficial Guide to Hot Careers.* New York: IDG Books Worldwide, 2000.

Goldberg, Jan. *Careers for Courageous People and Other Adventurous Types.* Lincolnwood, Ill.: VGM Career Horizons, 1997.

Hiam, Alexander. *Adventure Careers*. Hawthorne, N.J.: Career Press, 1995.

Kaplan, Andrew. *Careers for Outdoor Types*. Brookfield, Conn.: Millbrook Press, 1994.

Lee, Mary Price. *100 Best Careers in Crime Fighting: Law Enforcement, Criminal Justice, Private Security, and Cyberspace Crime Detection*. New York: IDG Books Worldwide, 1999.

Miller, Louise. *Careers for Nature Lovers and Other Outdoor Types*. Lincolnwood, Ill.: VGM Career Horizons, 1992.

HEAVY-DUTY RESOURCES

Career encyclopedias provide general information about a lot of professions and can be a great place to start a career search. Those listed here are easy to use and provide useful information about nearly a zillion different jobs. Look for them in the reference section of your local library.

Cosgove, Holli, ed. *Career Discovery Encyclopedia: 2000 Edition*. Chicago: J. G. Ferguson Publishing Company, 2000.

Hopke, William. *Encyclopedia of Careers and Vocational Guidance*. Chicago: J. G. Ferguson Publishing Company, 1999.

Maze, Marilyn, Donald Mayall, and J. Michael Farr. *The Enhanced Guide for Occupational Exploration: Descriptions for the 2,800 Most Important Jobs*. Indianapolis: JIST Works, 1995.

VGM's Career Encyclopedia. Lincolnwood, Ill.: VGM Career Books, 1997.

FINDING PLACES TO WORK

Use resources like these to find leads on local businesses, mentors, job shadowing opportunities, and internships. Later, use these same resources to find a great job!

Cubbage, Sue A. *National Job Hotline Directory*. River Forest, Ill.: Planning/Communications, 1998.

Graber, Steve. *Adams Jobs Almanac*. Holbrooke, Mass.: Adams Media Group, 1998.

———. *The Job Bank Guide to Computer and High Tech Companies*. Holbrooke, Mass.: Adams Media Group, 1997.

Levering, Robert. *100 Best Companies to Work for in America*. New York: Plume, 1994.

Peterson's Hidden Job Market. Princeton, N.J.: Peterson's Guides, 1998.

Peterson's Top 2500 Employers. Princeton, N.J.: Peterson's Guides, 1999.

Plunkett, Jack W. *The Almanac of American Employers*. Houston: Plunkett Research, 2000.

Potts, Kathleen E. Maki, ed. *Job Hunter's Sourcebook: Where to Find Employment Leads and Other Job Search Resources*. Detroit: Gale Research, Inc., 1999.

U.S. Department of Labor's Career Guide to America's Top Industries. Indianapolis: JIST Works, 1998.

Also consult the Job Bank series (Holbrook, Mass.: Adams Media Group). Adams publishes separate guides for Atlanta, Seattle, and many major points in between. Ask your local librarian if the library has a guide for the biggest city near you.

FINDING PLACES TO PRACTICE JOB SKILLS

An apprenticeship is an official opportunity to learn a specific profession by working side by side with a skilled professional. As a training method, it's as old as the hills, and it's making a comeback in a big way

because people are realizing that doing a job is simply the best way to learn a job.

An internship is an official opportunity to gain work experience (paid or unpaid) in an industry of interest. Interns are more likely to be given entry-level tasks but often have the chance to rub elbows with people in key positions within a company. In comparison to an apprenticeship, which offers very detailed training for a specific job, an internship offers a broader look at a particular kind of work environment.

Both are great ways to learn the ropes and stay one step ahead of the competition. Consider it dress rehearsal for the real thing!

Anselm, John. *The Yale Daily News Guide to Internships.* New York: Kaplan, 1999.

Oakes, Elizabeth H. *Ferguson's Guide to Apprenticeship Programs.* Chicago: J. G. Ferguson Publishing Company, 1998.

Oldman, Mark. *America's Top Internships.* New York: Princeton Review, 1999.

Peterson's Internships 2000. Princeton, N.J.: Peterson's Guides, 1999.

NO-COLLEGE OCCUPATIONS

Some of you will be relieved to learn that a college degree is not the only route to a satisfying, well-paying career. Whew! If you'd rather skip some of the schooling and get down to work, here are some books you need to consult.

Abrams, Kathleen S. *Guide to Careers Without College.* Danbury, Conn.: Franklin Watts, 1995.

Corwen, Leonard. *College Not Required: 100 Great Careers That Don't Require a College Degree.* New York: Macmillan, 1995.

Farr, J. Michael. *America's Top Jobs for People Without College Degrees.* Indianapolis: JIST Works, 1998.

Unger, Harlow G. *But What If I Don't Want to Go to College?: A Guide to Successful Careers through Alternative Education.* New York: Facts On File, 1998.

INDEX

Page numbers in **boldface** indicate main articles. Page numbers in *italics* indicate photographs.

neighbors 142
Neil, Alan W. 25–27, *25*
newspaper articles 142

O

officer, military 83
oil rigs 98
oil rig worker **97–104**
organizations and associations
142, 145
    airplane pilot 24–25
    astronaut 33
    carpenter 40
    commercial model 48
    computer security expert
56–57
    detective 64
    expedition leader 71–72
    firefighter 79
    military serviceperson 87
    miner 94–95
    oil rig worker 102
    paramedic 109–10
    ranch hand 114–15
    scuba diver 121–22
    welder 128

P

parafoil 32
paramedic **105–11**
parents 142
payload specialist 29
pen pals 147
Petit, Dan 123–24, *123*
petroleum engineer 97
pets 114

physical fitness
    firefighter and 75–76
    military and 84–85
    paramedic and 105, 108
pilot
    airplane **19–27**
    spacecraft 29, 30
pit truck driver 90
plane pilot **19–27**
police detective 60, 62
practice suggestions
    airplane pilot 19, 22, 23
    astronaut 28, 31–33
    carpenter 36, 38–39
    commercial model 43, 46
    computer security expert
      51, 55–56
    detective 60, 62–63
    expedition leader 67, 69, 70
    firefighter 75, 77
    military serviceperson 82,
      84–85
    miner 90, 92
    oil rig worker 97
    paramedic 105, 107–8
    ranch hand 112, 114
    scuba diver 118, 120
    welder 125, 127
    See also games; Internet
      sites; job training;
      volunteering
privacy, computer 53
private investigator (PI) 60, 61,
  65–66
private pilot 21
private pilot's license 21
professional associations *See*
  organizations and
  associations